Living a Bigger Life

Stop Dieting, Start Thriving

By Julie Creffield

Living A Bigger Life
Stop Dieting, Start Thriving

Copyright: Julie Creffield
Published: 1st October 2018
Edited by Becky Slack

The images in this book have been created or reimagined by the incredibly talented illustrator BootzMama who you can find on Instagram and Facebook, many of these can be downloaded from **www.juliecreffield.com/LBLresources** for your use alongside the book.

This book has been written with the belief that women of all sizes can enjoy sport and movement. It touches on mindset issues and past traumas which you may find triggering. If you have any concerns about your physical or mental health at any time while reading this book, please consult a doctor. The Author is not liable for any complications, injuries, loss or medical problems arising from or in connection with using this book.

Thank you for respecting the hard work of this author. Find out more at www.juliecreffield.com or on twitter @juliecreffield and Instagram @julie_creffield

—

I spent 20 years of my life trying not to be FAT

I am determined not to spend the next 20 years feeling like THAT

This one is for you Rose.

May you never feel inadequate or held back by the way you look.

Go be awesome.

What's in the Book?

Taking the First Step

"A marathon really does start with just one step"

As a plus-size endurance athlete, one of the most frequent questions I'm ever asked is: "How the hell do you run for six hours nonstop when you do your marathons?"

Now it's worth noting that this question is often asked by people who are in total disbelief after finding out:

A. That I actually run marathons (yes, I've run more than one)
B. That it takes me an average of six hours to complete them (sometimes more)

But I guess if you are not a runner yourself, or can't quite picture my size-18 body pounding the streets for 26.2 miles straight, it is a pretty reasonable enquiry to make.

I always respond in the same way.

 "It's easy, you just put one foot in front of the other and don't stop until someone puts a medal around your neck or you get carted off in an ambulance".

Now I know that is kind of a super flippant answer, and that there's obviously a more technical, and probably much more helpful response I could give, but it's true.

Marathons always start with a single step - and for the record, rarely end up with me being carted off by an ambulance, although I was knocked over by one during a 10K race at Leeds Castle once but the less said about that the better.

Marathon running is not as hard as you might think believe it or not.

I have always found that when it comes to running, it is the ability to run for 10 consecutive minutes without stopping that is the true battle. I know it might sound strange but by the time you are even considering training for a marathon, the lion's share of the hard work - both physically and mentally - has already been done; even if you are starting from scratch again after a break (something I often find myself doing)

Often the biggest challenge with anything like this is giving up in the early stages, letting your brain convince you that you can't do it, before giving your body the chance to prove to you otherwise.

Don't worry though ladies, this book is not about running.

Fear not. I won't be convincing anybody in this particular book that to live a BIG and purposeful life you have to embark on the crazy sport of long distance running or any other physical activity come to think of it. But don't let me stop you if all of a sudden you feel the urge. I know how infectious my enthusiasm for sporting challenges can be.

Anyway, I digress.

Marathons or no marathons, there is an almighty power struggle that goes on in your brain when you first embark on any kind of new self-development challenge, be that taking up running, starting a new yoga practice, or simply saying kinder things to yourself on a regular basis.

It's never the actual thing that is the thing; it's often the getting out of your own way to allow the thing to just kind of happen that is the tough part.

Right?

Having taken on all manor of BIG challenges over the last 10 years, I have always found huge power in stripping the challenge right back, not focusing on the hours and hours of practice ahead of you and instead simply breaking it down to the simplest of first steps. What do I need to do today? And how do I make sure I actually do it?

And so...

How do you start writing a book which you know has the power to change the life of the woman reading it, without overthinking it, without sounding like someone you are not, without chickening out and not writing the damn thing at all?

You start with sharing the most critical message of all, surely? Even if convention might dictate to save that until at least a quarter of the way through the book.

Well, here goes.

I know it sounds super cringey, and probably not the most profound way to start a self-help book like this one, but there is something I need to get off my chest, even though I know you're not going to believe me when I say it.

—

But it is a critical first step for you.

It was for me.

It is THE ONLY first step you even need to take on right now.

I know though that the second you read what I am about to say you are either going to roll your eyes like some kind of stroppy teenager being told that gum is bad for your gut or worse still, you will start thinking I am some kind of idiot who doesn't know what the hell she is talking about.

Imposter syndrome alert!!!

I have to start the book this way, I have to…I simply have to say what I need to say, because if you learn nothing more from this book, at least I know I told you this crucial fact right from the start and it didn't get lost anywhere along the way.

Because if you are anything like me, you sometimes, even with the best will in the world, launch into new books like this with great enthusiasm, only to come a cropper once you have to actually do some work or change your beliefs about something that has fundamentally enabled you to stay within your comfort zone for some time.

You too??

So yeah, I'm getting this in early, before you do some kind of dramatic u-turn, before you decide it's all too hard… before you lose yourself under the pressures you already have as a woman, without me adding to your mental load - and reading list.

You have been warned. I'm going in… I am going to tell you one of the key fundamental messages from this book, the single most powerful message that had been missing from my life that has single-handedly changed my life. Are you ready?

Wait for it… wait for it….

You.

Are.

Enough.

Yep, you heard me.

You are enough.

Just as you are today, reading this book. You are enough.

See, I told you.

I told you you would think I was some kind of dickhead.

Coz, it's hardly rocket science, is it?

I warned you that you might get a bit annoyed with me that we are actually going there with all of this "you just need to believe in yourself more" stuff. Yes, we are going there lovely, because unfortunately, we all need to be going there just a little more than we currently do.

This book is about Living Bigger.

It is about taking up space in this world.

But most of all, it is about accepting yourself exactly as you are right now for the awesome creation you are, and sticking your fingers up to the big bad world that constantly tells you that you are not good enough.

Fuck 'em.

(More about my persistent swearing habit a little later)

Living Bigger is about accepting that you are enough, but more than that, it is about deciding that you have had enough.

Enough of the unattainable demands the world puts on us women
Enough of the restraints we put on our own lives
Enough of the soul-destroying narrative that is constantly playing around being smaller

But as you well know, words alone do nothing in helping you get over the: "I am not enough" challenges you face every day; the never-ending monologue of reasons you can't do, be or have more in your life; the reason that you couldn't possibly do all those exciting things you once dreamed of doing.

This book is about action.

You took action in buying the god-damn thing, so let's build on that momentum and do some awesome shit together, OK?

Look, let's face it.

You have probably seen the "You are enough" or "You are perfect just as you are" statements in a billion internet memes, printed on mugs, T-shirts and other plastic tat, and perhaps you have heard other online coaches or social media influencers saying the very same thing in their bikini-clad posts.

And yet still you are not having any of it.

Well, you haven't until this point... well, not to the extent that you could.

You may agree with the sentiment of "feeling like you are enough", and in particular how it applies to other women in principle...but for you?

Nah...you're just not buying it.

If you were enough, you wouldn't be looking to the internet for answers, or buying yet another self-help book? If you were enough, you wouldn't always be thinking up new ways to make yourself feel better, look better and do better?

If you were enough, you wouldn't be questioning why you always feel so bloody awful, useless, stupid, alone, ugly, unattractive or insert any other self-limiting belief you have about yourself here.

I get it.

You don't believe me when I say it, and why should you?

I don't even know you.

Chances are I've never met you, so how can I be so sure of your "enoughness?", and even if I have met you in real life or online (it is possible, of course), I obviously don't know the real you, right? Just like you don't know the real me, because we are all so bloody good at putting on a front. Hiding the sides of ourselves that we know are unpalatable to the rest of the world?

Besides, the "I am not enough" message isn't always front of mind, is it? None of us proactively choose to lead with that thought about our self each day, because that would be stupid, right? The "I'm not enough" message is instead one of those insidious thoughts that somehow finds a way to sneak in, particularly when other things are not going right. When we have an argument with our partner; when the dress we were going to wear doesn't fit; when we get turned down for a job we really wanted...

That's when the annoying little voices start playing havoc in your mind.

So NO...you don't always feel like you are enough?

I get it, I get it.

So how about this?

Would it surprise you to know that when I first started writing this chapter, I actually wanted to use the word "perfect" instead of "enough"?

Imagine that?

Too much? What do you reckon? I know right? What was I thinking?

It's OK though, don't worry I came to my senses shortly after typing it out right at the start of this chapter and seeing the absolute ridiculousness of it before my own eyes.

You see, I thought (and perhaps still think) that the idea of you being perfect might push you over the edge, just like it pushed me over the edge (I actually closed the laptop and had a little meltdown at that point - who did I think I was even beginning to write this book when I couldn't decide on the right word to even describe the women that would be reading it?).

I mean come on, nobody's perfect right?

And as women, boy oh boy how dare we even suggest that we are anything close to perfection, how very dare we. Especially us FAT women. YES, I WENT THERE!!! I know, I know. Less than a couple of pages in and I have already used the F word. What can I say, I love F words (but more of that later).

Perfect was the word I really want to use though, and before I started looking up the dictionary definition of it (because that's what us writers sometimes do) I was convinced it was the right word, because my intention was to remind you of just how wonderful you are. I wanted to start this book by giving you a gift, and we all know you should never look a gift horse in the mouth, right?

"Oh you look lovely," says the nice friend who notices your new dress.
"Oh really," you reply, feeling all weirded out by the compliment.
"Yes, that dress really suits you, it's perfect," they add.
"Urgghh, I'm not sure, it was in the sale on ASOS and it kinda fits so I decided to keep it. I'm not sure though, I think I look fat in it," you reply.
"No, you don't look fat, you look lovely," they say.

Yeah, because being fat and looking great are mutually exclusive after all.

What if the outfit was indeed perfect, but you just couldn't see it? What if you were constructing flaws because it is easier and more comfortable to do that? Because, if it was perfect, you would have to acknowledge your role in its perfectness.

OK.

Let me stop for a moment, or hold my horses as my nan used to say.

Can I just ask a favour?

You know when you've got a good friend, like a bloody brilliant friend? Someone who is always there for you, makes you feel really good about yourself, never lets you down? Is just a good egg?

Do you have one of them?

Good.

Well, have they ever said something to you that you just didn't agree with? Like an opinion on something, or a value that just doesn't sit well with yours? Nothing major where you would consider ending the friendship, but it just stops you in your tracks for a short while as you get used to the fact you don't truly understand all aspects of them? That you don't see eye to eye on EVERYTHING like you thought you did.

And so what do you do?

Well, because they are your friend and not some random person, you just park the idea or the conversation, and you agree to disagree, right? Because you trust that the ongoing relationship is more important than that little detail.

Well, can I ask you to kind of do the same thing with me, here?

Because I know you don't really know me, and this book hasn't really got into its flow yet. So can I ask for you to bear with me and give me the benefit of doubt for a bit? Just until we really get stuck into the juicy chapters? Perhaps where you get to trust me a bit more, and see there is some method to my madness?

Yeah?

Think of it like date number two with a new love interest. Like they were attractive/interesting/funny enough to want to find out more about them after your first encounter, but let's just say you are not exactly cancelling your Tinder account or telling your Mum about him (or her) just yet?

Right, back to the book.

So yeah, I did want to use the word Perfect, I really did.

But do you know why I couldn't use it? Because if I tried to convince you the reader that you are perfect, I would have to convince myself "the writer" that I was too, and when the dictionary definition started talking about concepts like "flawless" and without "error", I was like, "nope, let's stick with 'Enough'".

Because the thought of prancing around in anything even remotely resembling perfectness scared the shit out of me.

I could just imagine my mum, my siblings, my ex-partner, and my school teachers literally laughing until they cried at this very idea. I had thoughts of all those moments in my past where I behaved nowhere near perfectly, and people such as my old boss, my neighbours, the people I sometimes get into pointless rows online with thinking about the sheer audacity I have of saying this out loud about myself - and this is before we get onto any thoughts relating to the far-from-perfect body I live in with its unruly cellulite, numerous rolls of flab, and carelessly chipped finger nails.

Perfect as an idea is just too damn provocative.

But what a bloody shame that it is.

What if all of us were perfect? What if how we are is exactly how we should be. Like in some matrix-style, butterfly effect, final destination kinda way, and that this constant unease with our self is actually responsible for many of the modern diseases that so many of us women around the world are trying to come to terms with.

What if it is our perfect imperfectness that is keeping the planet spinning on its axis, and that somehow our uncomfortableness with this and our constant pursuit of perfection (even though it already exists) is what is causing so much unhappiness within our species?

Deep, hey?

If you are at all religious in any way or maybe even spiritual, you might find it somewhere deep within yourself to make a connection to having been created as a perfect being of sorts, born in the image of God (good old Catholic upbringing here).

Is it too far of a leap to believe in the idea of perfection being something you already are in your very existence, rather than something to constantly have to strive for?

Well, consider this?

Were we not all born into this world and deemed as absolutely perfect at some point?

I'm hazarding a guess that I was - even if my mum would rather poke needles in her eyes than tell me so. I tried for the purposes of this book to get her to say it, I really did, but it was just too big an ask. God only knows what would have happened if I had asked her to think of herself as perfect back in 1955 when she arrived on this planet.

So in the absence of any reassurance from my parents (my dad is out of the picture so couldn't ask him to back up my theory either) I am just going to assume that I was in fact a perfect baby girl when I first made my appearance into this world back in 1978, even if I was born with a very dark birthmark on my left leg – something that continues to remind me, every time someone says "Oh what's that on your leg", that I am in some ways flawed.

But I digress.

You would have been considered perfect too, right?

———

Pretty much all of us in the first few minutes, hours or days of our life, had our parents, doctors and nurses, wider family, and then even absolute strangers in the street gaze at us adoringly, making all kind of fuss over just how perfect we were?

Did we fight that idea of perfection?

Did we heck? We lapped it up.

We gazed back at those who stared at us, we slept blissfully through all the cuddles, stroking and pampering we had inflicted on us. We revelled in the idolisation, and the knowledge that we had parents waiting on us hand and foot. We only needed to gurgle, cough or fart in the early days and someone would race to make sure we were OK. For goodness sake they even checked on us when we were asleep to make sure we were still alive.

Imagine someone doing that for us now?

I reckon I could go quiet for a week and nobody would much notice.

It's kind of sad that it all stopped really, not the checking that we are still alive bit because that would be creepy. Oh fuck, perhaps we still have that to come as we head towards our graves?

But seriously ladies, maybe it's about time we brought at least some of it back.

The irony with all of this is that in many ways we were living so much bigger when we were physically smaller. As babies, we instinctively embraced everything that made us unique; we loved ourselves so completely, and we knew without doubt that we were the most important person on the planet. Why do you think as toddlers we were obsessed with our reflections? We were bloody gorgeous that's why - even if some of us were chubby, bald, spotty, or snotty...we didn't care and neither did anyone else.

Where did we lose that self-belief, self-admiration? Was it as a result of others highlighting our flaws? Was it when we started comparing ourselves to others, or was it when we started to be influenced by external forces such as the media? And is there anything at all we can do go back to that idyllic state?

Perhaps we need to reclaim our ability to be perfect in our imperfections once again? Perhaps we need to renew our ability to be enough, with or without a desire for more?
Perhaps we just need to be a little kinder to ourselves?

One of my all-time favourite internet memes (and trust me I have a few that I like) is the one that states:

"You can be a masterpiece and a work in progress at the same time."

It is so true.

We are led to believe that it has to be one or the other, that the end goal is perfection and that the stuff along the way is neither worthy of highlighting nor good enough in and of itself. It is hardly any wonder that we spend so much of our lives weighing up seemingly opposing concepts, such as "body confidence" and "beach body ready"?

Maybe it is not about the pursuit of perfection, or for argument's sake, the idea of being enough, but instead is about finding an ability to accept the concept of perfection or enoughness like they are absolute givens, and that it would be ridiculous and plain right rude to believe otherwise.

Look, I know I have thrown you in at the deep end here with all this self-acceptance and, dare I say it, self-love stuff so early in the book. But sorry lovely, you need it. I need it. We all bloody well need it. More so than ever. Even if you don't feel like you need it or want it for yourself, we need it to empower future generations of women, because if we carry on the way we are, it won't be global warming, alien invasion or nuclear war bringing the word as we know it to its knees. It will be our own ability to self-destruct and hate on ourselves that will do it for us.

So yes, to a certain extent I am saying the future of woman (and I guess man) kind is in your hands, and if you can't do it for you, at least hear me out so that you can pass on some of these ideas to other women in your life.

This is a book about women living the "bestest" version of themselves, whatever that looks like for each of us. It is about questioning the status quo of the female experience, both the collective and the individual, and it is about empowering you to live your life however you wish.

Can I share a story with you?

I don't believe I am living my BIGGEST life yet, but what I do know is I am well on my way towards it, and before I draw this opening chapter to an end, I would like to share a critical story with you which will hopefully illustrate the power that living bigger can have if you are brave enough to go after it.

I love a good old story me, and by the end of this book hopefully you will too.

Back in July 2018 (just a few months before this book was completed) I did something that even by my standards was pretty scary.

It was something I had wanted for a while, something I knew was in my future, but never the less once I had it within my reach I was absolutely terrified of fucking it up.

I will never forget that feeling as I stood backstage in that darkened auditorium, at that swanky new theatre space in Folkestone, Kent. It was truly like having an out-of-body experience, and I could only imagine how scary it must have been for the speakers who were speaking in front of a live audience for the first time.

I had all the clichéd signs of fear. A dry mouth, sweaty palms, a pounding heart… but the thing that annoyed me most was an almost Hollywood-style muffled movie soundtrack. Seriously, for a while I wondered if I had actually gone deaf, or was suffering sudden and unexplained hearing problems as I struggled to hear anything other than my insecurities playing out in my brain.

I had months to prepare, which also meant that I had months to over-analyse it all and build it up in my mind.

I had advice and support from some of my incredible speaker friends, and speaker coaches had listened to the talk I had prepared and given great feedback, and yet still I stood there knowing that the only line I knew with any level of certainty was the opening line:

"Running your first marathon is like having your first baby, you know it's going to hurt, you just don't know how much."

The day before rehearsals, in the theatre space with the un-ironed circle of red carpet and technicians still rigging the lights, had been an absolute disaster. I couldn't remember any of it, and the lovely lady with my script as a prompt did her best to help me through it, but all I could think was:

"Julie, you bloody idiot…what a wasted opportunity."

And so with that damn red carpet with its spotlight jeering at me and the ever so sweet Compare cheerfully introducing me as the next speaker, I took one final breath and mouthed the words: "Julie you are enough… whatever happens on that stage, it will be enough."

And I stepped on to that stage and delivered the only talk I could possibly have delivered on that day.

Was it perfect? Did I say everything in the order I wanted to or include everything that should have been in there? Nope. I ummed, I ahhed, I probably had a few moments where I scrambled around for the next few lines, and maybe even repeated myself, but despite all of these issues, I did something millions of people simply couldn't, or simply wouldn't be able to do.

I delivered a TEDx talk.

I stood in front of a live audience as the final speaker of the day, with a set of video cameras recording a 16-minute talk which would stay with me for life... like seriously guys, FOREVER.

I did the only thing I could do. My best.

And do you know the worst thing about recording a TEDx talk? There is no going back. The talk you give is the talk you give is the talk you give. There is no editing, there is no tweaking, no deleting, no second chances.

In the aftermath of the talk, and the eight long weeks it took to see a recording of it, I 100% made my peace with the fact it wasn't perfect. The irony being the talk was about the fear of judgement, the fear of people thinking badly because of how you look or come across to them.

All the stress I had put myself under about what to wear, how to do my hair, what stories to tell, which not to... None of it mattered. I stood on that stage in my Primark jeans, with my split ends, and a foundation stain on my red jacket (that sure as hell wasn't my finest moment in the changing room 10 minutes before my talk).

I stood on that stage unapologetically as me.

The process of putting my imperfect self out there for the world to see was the catalyst I desperately needed to get on with writing this book, to get on with spreading my message to the women of the world that they are enough. And most importantly to get on with living the biggest, bestest life I can lead.

If you have seen THAT video what you might see is a confident, capable woman, delivering the talk of her life in a red jacket and a crisp white blouse. What you didn't see was the frantic woman just 15 minutes earlier trying to get foundation out of the white vest, and re-straightening her hair due to some weird early-menopausal excessive sweating.

If you haven't seen the talk yet, you can check it out here **http://bit.ly/JuliesTEDx** or over on my YouTube channel **https://www.youtube.com/juliecreffield**

So welcome to my world, ladies.

It might not always be slick, or pretty, but it sure as hell is real and dare I say it a little bit awesome at times.

And no, that is not showing off. That's showing up for myself, and acknowledging my unique talents and power as a woman. Just as how I hope you will in time too.

Welcome to the world of #Iblamejulie

So just a word on this hashtag...because you may be reading that and thinking...well, that's bit egotistical.

I thought the same the first time I saw it.

In fact, I ignored it and hoped it would go away.

The "I blame Julie" hashtag was started around two years ago in my online running club, The Clubhouse.

A woman went out and ran further than she ever had and came back and posted in the group using the hashtag, as a nod to the influence I had had on her journey to this point.

I laughed.

Other women laughed.

They commented on it being a great hashtag.

I cringed a bit.

I hoped it would never be used again

But it was.

Women started using the hashtag for all kinds of reasons

- Just signed up for a race
- Just tried out a new fitness class
- Woke up with sore muscles
- Applied for a new job
- Bought new clothes

It started to take on a life of its own, on social media.

Yet still I was reluctant to use it.

It was a bit like I was blowing my own trumpet.

I hadn't yet stepped into my power, my self belief, my trust in myself as an influencer, an encourager, a coach...I was still worried about what people would think of me. Like I was getting too big for my boots.

But the women loved it.

They felt like posting about their accomplishments using this hashtag that they were part of a movement.

Like it meant something not only to them, but as a reminder to all women that you can achieve all sorts of things with the support of other women behind you.

I started to feel the same.

I realised as I sat down to write this book, that I couldn't omit it. I couldn't pretend this wasn't an important part of my work.

But it just shows you how quick we are to hide our light.

So I have included the story of how it came about, to illustrate that sometimes we have to be brave, we have to be visible, we have to let others be inspired by us...even if it sometimes feels a bit weird or uncomfortable.

So come on in, pull up a pew...I'll put the kettle on.

Oh and can I just congratulate you on taking another first step, you actually read the first chapter of this book. Do you know how many women buy self-help books and never bloody read them?

How To Use This Book?

"What have you got to lose? Well, about three stone, seeing as you are asking"

First things first.

This is NOT A DIET BOOK.

You know, like those books that say they are anti-dieting and then half way through tell you what the fuck to eat and how much to exercise? Yeah, this is not one of those books.

I promise.

It's not even an ANTI DIET BOOK really...because even I don't have the strength to fight the magnitude of support there still is for competitive dieting among women.

No. This is more of a Ladies, CAN WE PLEASE TALK ABOUT SOMETHING OTHER THAN FLIPPING DIETING FOR A WHILE???, so we can get on with doing other awesome stuff with our lives kinda book.

Even if it is just for a little while, a tiny interlude, some much-needed respite. It is time to take a break.

The not-dieting thing is only a small part of this book, so if you are still very much in that dieting space, don't worry there is still a whole heap more you can get from the book if you are not quite ready to cancel your diet club subscription yet.

It's a small part, but it does require a mahousive mindset shift. So I am not even for one moment believing that this book alone will convince everyone that reads it to ditch their dieting tools, attitudes, and actions.

But it is a starter for conversation at least.

For me, the non-dieting piece was the final part of the jigsaw in terms of turning my life around when I literally couldn't have been any more unhappy with myself. I will be talking about my experience of dieting and how it has shaped who I am, and what it has taken to finally accept myself at whatever size my body happens to be, and to get on with being just a little bit awesome each day.

The quote at the beginning of this chapter? Well, that was line from a stand-up comedy gig I did a few years back. It got an almighty laugh, but looking at it now I cringe that I actually felt that it was OK to make fun of myself in this way.

19

But more about how I use humour to mask my true feelings later.

If this book is not about dieting, what else can you expect in it?

Technically speaking, this is the eighth book I have self-published. But in many ways it feels like it is my first. I am more nervous about this one than I have ever been with any of the others because for the first time in my career I am not just writing about my experiences of running, or my way of doing things... but instead I am pretty much laying myself bare for everyone to see.

Putting myself up there for criticism, putting myself up there for critique.

And it is scary.

With this book I have tried to use my Living Bigger philosophies in the actual development of the book, taking each creative decision and asking myself, am I going BIG enough with this? Am I holding anything back? Am I playing small or taking the easy option? Could I be bolder, braver, more ambitious?

For example, in my previous books, I have often started my chapters by quoting other women I admire, with carefully constructed pieces of advice fitting to the content of that segment. But with this book I decided to be my own role model, and not give away my power so easily. I have something to share of my own at the start of each chapter.

So yeah, I am 100% in the driving seat this time round.

Don't get it twisted though ladies, I haven't completely got my shit together. Seriously. I have to remind myself not to be an idiot all of the time. I often make mistakes and have to be like "yeah, next time Julie, let's not do it that way, OK". I am going to be honest in this book about the stuff I still find hard, the stuff I still need to work on, because hopefully you will identify with some of this, and maybe start backing yourself more too, instead of needing to be the finished article before stepping up.

And a word about the swearing?

Maybe I should have written a disclaimer a little earlier in the book. I like to swear. Not because it makes me feel big or clever, or helps me to fit in with the cool people online who swear. But because it absolutely is part of who I am, and it is not something I am ready to give up yet.

If you met me in real life it's unlikely I would swear in a professional setting, nor around your kids and rarely do I swear on stage when I am giving a talk (unless I am about to fall of the bleeding thing). But spend any time with me socially, or get me talking about something that really gets my goat and yes I may swear.

I try to limit the really aggressive swear words because I know they offend, but equally I don't want to censor myself. It has taken me a long while to like myself, and if you don't like me because I swear then that's fine by me.

Different strokes, different folks.

Oh and just for the record...I don't like Marmite OK?

So, how should you approach this book?

First.

Nobody likes being told how to read a book, right? It should be common sense. I know it might sound a little obvious but read it cover to cover. There really is no point in flicking through to find the "How to" bit to speed up the process.

Have you ever done that with diet books? Like enough of the "why it works" filler just tell me what to flipping eat and what not to eat already.

You may wish to read it through once and then stop and think about how to implement, or you may wish to take your time and go through each task one by one. You know yourself better than I do, do what works for you. But remember you are only cheating yourself if you don't try some of the exercises and tasks that I suggest throughout.

Remember, these are things I get women like you to do in my coaching groups. Women who at the start had huge resistance to doing the work, every excuse under the sun for why these techniques wouldn't work for them, but who have experienced incredible transformations as a result.

Within this book, you will obviously find a lot of my views on the world as I see it for women in the western world right now. Lots of anecdotal stories from the women I have worked with over the years, plus the lived experiences that have shaped me and my work. But most importantly, and this is super, super important for me, I am including a range of practical tools and solutions to the multitude of problems we face as women.

So use them.

I didn't want this just to be me on my soapbox putting the world to rights, you can head over to my YouTube channel or check out my bazillion backdated blog posts for that, right? No, I wanted to give you stuff that was actually helpful. That you could put into practice right away.

LIKE NOW!!!!!

You can start using these tools and techniques to help you make the BIG or small changes you want to make in your life, starting now, this very moment. Or you can choose to do nothing. But change will only come if you choose to take action.

Let me be upfront with you. I am going to need you to do some shit here. At times, some of this will be really deep and challenging. I can't do it for you and I sure as hell can't guarantee you it is going to be stuff you will want to do.

Please don't read a great exercise in this book and think: "oh yeah, I'll do that in a bit." You won't do it. I know you won't. Seriously. I am going to need you to approach this book like it was a flipping Masters degree - buy a new folder, post-it notes and some pens (ooooh stationery) and carve out time in your week to do the bloody work.

I know all too well how tempting it is to believe that somehow by the power of osmosis the words from this book are going to seep into your brain and by some kind of magic, change everything you have ever believed about yourself and the world that you live in.

If you are an old hat at self-development work, you will know that it is real work and you can't just play lip service to it. If you are new to it: welcome, my darling, strap yourself in and don't be surprised if the journey gets a little bumpy.

Can I pre-warn you about something?

I am known affectionately by my clients as the "no bullshit life coach", I am the life coach for women that don't do life coaching, and I can tell you, I ain't got time for bullshit, yours or mine for that matter. I wasted too many years blaming and shaming everyone for the stuff that I needed to sort out, and I am not about to start wasting time on yours.

I will call you out on your bullshit, just as I call myself out on mine. EVERY. SINGLE. DAY.

I have a big bright buzzer on my desk for this very purpose. I bought it off Amazon as I thought it would make a good prop for Instagram photos and maybe even workshops I run, but I actually just use it when I'm in my office.

It's great.

Whenever I find myself making up unhelpful stories, feeling remotely sorry for myself, or generally not doing the important stuff I know deep down I want to do, I reach for my buzzer and I push the damn thing (it's just as well that I live by myself, hey?).

It says the following phrases:

"*siren wails* Bullshit detected, take precautions *siren wails*"
"*ding dong* Bullshit in aisle two"
"Buuuuuuuuuuullllsssshhiiiit"
"*Industrial honk* That was bullshit"
"Warning, warning bullshit alert"

And my overall favourite:

"Bullshit" said with a cockney accent.

The thing is, we are not that good at calling out our own bullshit, are we ladies? We are too busy thinking about our flaws and shortcomings in a "oh, it's all so hard" or "but it's all their fault" kind of way.
It's either hold on to your bullshit or open yourself up to growth - you can't really do both.

Don't get me wrong. I say this with love because I know I did this for far too many years myself, everything was everyone else's fault. I didn't want to do the work and I didn't want to take any responsibility for the role I had played in who I had become. I now have some wonderful techniques for dumping these unhelpful habits.

But it's all good. We are in this together, well at least for the duration of you working through this book – a book I wrote with one very clear intention.

To help you feel better about yourself.

Each and every time I got stuck, lost confidence, questioned the will to live during the planning, writing and editing stages of this book, I stopped to simply asked myself the question?

"Why are you writing this book, Julie?"

And the answer each time was:

"To help women feel better about themselves"

Any why was this so important, you ask?

Because ultimately I spent 20 years of my life wanting to feel better about myself. Twenty years of my life trying not to be FAT. Twenty years trying to understand what was wrong with me, why I was so unhappy.

This is the book I wish I could have read at age 16. This is the book I want to be able to give to my teenage nieces who probably look at me like some kind of weirdo, so that they can one day better understand that perhaps they are not weird themselves...or are perhaps wonderfully weird.

I wrote this book because ultimately I don't want women to feel as lonely as I have over the years. I don't mean lonely in terms of not having anyone to hang out with or confide in, because I have had plenty of that over the years. What I mean is the loneliness you feel when you truly believe you are the only person who has ever felt the way you do about yourself right now.

Trust me, you are not alone.

You are not.

There are thousands, maybe millions of women feeling exactly like you do right now.

But here's the thing.

Reading a book can be somewhat of a solitary pursuit. You sit with the ideas all by yourself, you don't always apply them into your real life, and its hard to find people on the same page when it comes to making the changes. OK, so sometimes you might recommend a good book to a friend, discuss it in passing, or maybe even get involved in some online discussion about its contents...but what I am needing to happen as a result of this book is a stonking great revolution.

A revolution which stopped us all from feeling so weird about wanting to change things? One where we encourage each other to become more self aware, to fight a bigger cause?

For example, what if there was a rule that stipulated this book could not be read in isolation? That it could only be read with someone else supporting you through it? That the paperback version was only ever bought in pairs? That the reading of the book was something to be enjoyed among peers, with sisters, between mother and daughters (more about this later).

What do you reckon?

I have realised over the years that one of the things that seems to be missing so much from our lives both women and men is a sense of connection. I mean REAL connection. Seth Godin talks about this in his book *Tribes*, when he describes the power the internet has had in allowing us to find connection in an otherwise fragmented world.

We are able more than ever to find solace and friendships in our obscure hobbies, beliefs and quirks, and it has changed everything. I grew an online business out of a need for overweight women to have somewhere they could come together to talk about being an overweight runner. Sometimes they didn't even want to discuss running or fitness, they just wanted to be together and to know somehow that other people like them exist.

There is a bit of a problem with this though.

Many of us (me included) have replaced some of our more traditional relationships with these more transient, fleeting, virtual ones, and we have increased the volume of these connections significantly, which can lower the quality of real-life interactions.

We literally have thousands of digital friends available to like our social media posts and help source information about the best lipsticks, while the time and space we have available to really take time to talk about the important stuff, to truly understand each other, has become less and less.

Even when we do manage to spend time with real-life friends, it is often to mark occasions, or to do specific things, to tick goals or travel destinations off lists. We rarely get the time to just be, to talk, to explore, to touch base with the deeper and maybe even darker versions of ourselves, that rarely come out to play.

Often I wonder if we even know some of our friends, or we are simply too lazy, too scared to question their foundations in case we are forced to upgrade them.

I hope to use this book, and the Living Bigger movement to change all of that. To give women a mechanism that uses the power of discussion to enable them to reconnect to each other and themselves. We talk a good game on social media, don't we? We talk about finding our tribe and lifting each other up, but how many of us find ourselves at a complete loss when we really need someone to talk something through or are struggling with our mental health?

Therefore, throughout the book you are going to find a number of "Check and Challenge" tasks. These can be done alone, virtually with others, or in what I like to call a Live Bigger "Knees Up" or "Nights In" which you can find out about at the end of the book.

Don't get me wrong, you need to work on your own shit before trying to mobilize the troupes to work on theirs. My vision for this Living Bigger work is for these tools and techniques to be commonplace ideas, replacing the sometimes meaningless chit chat of how to lose weight, how to get rid of cellulite, how to get the husband to clean the bath tub, kind of rubbish we often resort to.

So there is work to do. This is not a "read the book and all will be good in the world" kind of a book. I am relying on you to do your bit.

But wait a minute. Who the hell am I, anyway?

Why should you do anything I say? How can you know to trust me, when you barely know me, when you don't yet know my story, or at least not all of it?

In Chapter 7, I am going to be talking to you about the power of understanding your personal story, but before then I guess I could share with you a bit of mine. Not the deep emotional stuff, but more the narrative of how I got to be writing this book and why I am even qualified to be giving you advice or coaching.

My name is Julie Michelle Creffield, and I am a born and bred East Londoner.

I describe myself as a transformational life coach, fitness influencer, writer and speaker, but none of those things really feel like they do me justice. If anything, they serve just as a way of validating myself somehow...like without them I am a nobody.

I am a triathlete, a marathon runner and now even an ultramarathon runner, a stand-up comic, a TEDx speaker, I have a first-class degree and a Masters...some might call me an over-achiever.

I also happen to be a single parent to a beautiful mixed-race daughter, sister to five siblings, and daughter to my long-suffering mum.

I am a friend, a neighbour, a colleague, a peer.

I am also, as it currently stands, single.

Think you know who I am yet?

Trust me, I am still working on this too, so don't worry. I am only a few steps ahead of you when it comes to working this all out for myself.

Some would say I have had long enough to work out who I want to be when I grow up. Perhaps that's the problem. I am not quite ready to grow up and properly submerse myself in the adulting game.

The year I came up with the original concept, wrote and then published this book, I also happened to turn 40 and something major shifted within me. Divine planning or just coincidence do you reckon?

Now I know a lot of women talk about stepping into their power as they get older in years, but I believe this was something else. This wasn't about reaching a milestone birthday and finally growing up. This was about the multitude of adjustments I had been making in my life over the period of about five years (possibly since the birth of my daughter) all coming to a head and me finally having the clarity and courage to notice the shift and not be scared of it.

Most people in the online world or media know me as a plus-size marathon runner, the brains behind The Fat Girls Guide to Running blog, or the Too Fat to Run movement. But believe it or not I actually had a life before this role, a life that was equally challenging, demanding and exciting.

But it was a simple fitness blog charting the highs and lows of being an overweight endurance athlete that changed my life, and trust me I don't say those words lightly.

The blog changed everything for me.

Having always enjoyed writing as a way of expressing myself, I believe it was the first time in my adult life that I actually found my true voice.

The fact that I was able to be so open and honest about my fatness was a godsend, because up until that point, I had simply been in denial about what a crucial part of my identity it had been, and how desperately I was fighting against my body in a battle over what size it should be.

I now know that battle was futile.

I didn't need to fight it.

The problem is you don't know what you don't know until you do know, and then sometimes it takes a while for you to acknowledge that you now know something different. Therefore, you can be and do different, if of course you now want to.

Over the past five years I have coached more than 10,000 women. Shit that is a hell of a lot of women….and no that was not a pun. I once used to tell the joke:

"You could say I have a large female following"
"I do"
"I call her Brenda"
"She follows me around all of my races bringing me Vaseline for my chub rub"

You will find I often use humour to make sense of the things which I have struggled in the past to talk about in any other palatable format. This is something I am working on - getting the balance between being funny and entertaining, but not to the point of throwing myself and my fellow women under the bus.

That number - 10,000 women – that is true. In fact, it's probably an underestimation. I never actually started counting, but when I sat down once and actually totted it all up I was amazed at the number. Through my original blog, my various books on running, my online fitness programmes, my health and happiness retreats and in recent years my life coaching, I have supported tens of thousands of women.

This kind of work changes you as a woman, maybe as a male coach too, but as a female, I defy you to work on a deep emotional supportive level with women in this way and not be moved by it.

At times I have been overwhelmed with the enormity of the problems and challenges we face, and then at other times I have been in complete awe at just how resilient, supportive and inspiring we can be too.

And to think, I never set out to be a life coach either. Who does?

I never even set out to work with women specifically. I started my career working with young people, often teenage lads who were in trouble with the police, and completely disengaged from life as we know it.

Looking back, I don't even know how I did that job. What did I know about being a teenage boy living in a tower block, under enormous peer pressure, just trying to survive day-to-day in the best way he knew how?

I remember as a recent graduate I had this burning desire to help people, over and above any desire to actually sort out my own life, if truth be known. At the heart of this, was a need to be needed, a want to be wanted, a love of being loved.

I can see that now.

I am now able to see that as a strength, rather than as a weakness.

You see I have realised in the last few years that I have a weird ability to see the best in people. To see things in themselves that they are unable to see (things I sometimes even struggle to see in myself), and I am able to find solutions and ways forward for people who feel stuck, maybe because I have needed to find those very solutions in my own life.

Very little of what I know or think about coaching has come from any text book, or specific coaching techniques taught on a course. My processes, tools and techniques are devised often with simple common sense, and from having an adventurous curious nature.

I am extremely lucky to have had the life experiences I have had to bring me to this point. I am lucky that I have always had a desire to understand what makes people tick, and ultimately how we make this world a better place, while at the same time being ridiculously down to earth and realistic about how shitty life can be sometimes.

I understand all of these about myself because I believe that without a constant practice (and it is a practice, just like yoga or ballet is) of self-awareness, it is near on impossible to reach your potential and impact positively on the rest of the world.

We all know people who walk through life completely blinkered. Closed off to the impact they have to those around them; and if not blinkered, then with some weird frame of reference about how they think and behave and its effect on others. Maybe that is you? Maybe you don't want to look too close to home or maybe you know that it is time to do exactly that.

Do not get me wrong for even a moment. As Tony Robbins so helpfully put it in his recent documentary: I AM NOT YOUR GURU!!!

Hell no.

The moment I let my ego get so inflated that I start calling myself a GURU, or think that I am here to save the world, save your world, save you, please tell me what a twat I am being.

I am just me.

Nothing more nothing less.

I was going to say little old me, but that would be somewhat inaccurate. It does however illustrate my desire to quantify and belittle myself, it's a habit I have become super aware of since doing this work.

I am not a guru, but I am here to share with you the things that have changed my world, the things that have saved me (mainly from myself, I must add).

However, I absolutely do not do this as a standalone act. The way I see it is there is an army of incredibly talented and gifted women standing up around the world (often online) and reclaiming their power as change makers, holding space for other women to learn, to grow, and ultimately to be brilliant.

I am one voice in all of that.

An important one in the context of this book, but just one nether the less.

Some of what you read in this book you may have heard before. This does not mean I am copying the ideas, thoughts or views of anyone in particular. It just means that many concepts around personal development are rehashed simply by virtue of the amount of information we have available to us.

There is no such thing as a completely new idea right?

But there are new messengers and new ways of delivering messages. And you as individuals are more receptive to some of those than others. Such as in the same way as how your science teacher at school could give you some advice that is identical to that your drama teacher gave you, but you liked your drama teacher more, she used words that resonated with you better, and you sensed that she cared more about you actually implementing them.

It's that
You might have read heaps of Louise Hay, Wayne Dyer, Gabrielle Bernstein, Brene Brown or even Tony Robbins, and perhaps even attended their seminars, but alongside this you needed to hear this message from an overweight, middle-aged, working-class woman who doesn't always use big words, or look like her life is completely sorted yet.

Or maybe you are someone who doesn't do "self-help", and couldn't think of anything worse than having to listen to the thoughts of a "life coach", let alone be challenged to do stuff. Trust me I come across lots of women like that, who start off in my workshops with their arms crossed, determined not to laugh at my jokes or buy into my ideas. Then 20 minutes in, they can't help themselves and find themselves happily chatting to their neighbours about their wildest dreams.

I had so much resistance to writing this book because of the fear of judgement - the irony being that this is ultimately a book about the fear of judgement, FFS. I worried that I would do it a disservice, that I would do you a disservice, that I wouldn't be able to express myself clearly enough, or that someone else would come along and do it better.

And then I stopped and I took a breath and reminded myself of why I needed to get this book out of my head and into your hands NOW!!!

Simply put: I might not be here tomorrow and neither might you.

I'm not just talking about getting hit by a bus, although that too is possible. I am talking more about the pace in which this world changes, how thoughts change, movements happen, world events shape our understanding of the world.

Yes, I could have waited for a proper publisher to pick up my manuscript and decide it was worthy of publishing, and then wait the almost two years it takes to go to print, but the world would have moved on.
We haven't got time to waste.

It is this that started me off on this journey in the first place.

I was doing some research for my TEDx talk (the same TEDx talk that I applied for without truly knowing what I would talk about) and as I spent a few days trying to come up with my one idea worth sharing, I came across a quote that almost floored me.

"The average woman in the UK will spend 31 years of her life on a diet"

31 fucking years.

Apologies for the swearing there but come on people, it's outrageous. For some women that is literally half of their lives. Shit, some women will never know a life that doesn't involve dieting.

I wondered for many years if I would ever reach the point where my life didn't involve dieting? And when I had my daughter back in 2013, I worried that my relationship with food and my body would impact negatively on my daughter's, just as my mum's had me, and possibly even her mum's before her something it appears is quite common with many of the women I work with.

We will come back to the idea of dieting and the tricky mother daughter relationship that so many of us have endured later in the book as it needs a whole lot more dissecting, but for now I just need you to understand one simple driver for me.

I do not want my daughter wasting even one year of her life on the pursuit of smallness.

This is what we are talking about here. This is not about health or healthcare, this is not about longevity of life, or even happiness – although all of these things are important too. This is about a longstanding belief that to be a woman you must be attractive, and to be attractive you must be slim.

And I call bullshit on this idea.

I cannot stand back, knowing what I know, without speaking out on it.

This book needed to be written now, because I don't want any more of our valuable time being wasted when there is so much to be done in the world, by and for women, both on a collective and personal level.

And I know my methods are powerful in their ability to change lives positively.

I have seen first-hand women absolutely transform their life in a matter of days. The change is phenomenal to witness, and it is infectious. Once that desire for change is embedded, it never ceases to amaze me how quickly and profoundly things can shift, and how many other women are inspired when they see this happen for others around them.

Much of this change happens when women invest time and money in their own self-development. But more importantly, it happens when they decide they are worthy of prioritising their own needs.

One of the clients from my first ever life-coaching course gave me great belief in my work when she sent me a message saying:

"I didn't realise how much I wanted to change until I started - and now I don't want to stop changing."

Believe me when I say this can happen for you too: if you have that desire for change; if you have a desire to feel better; if the way your life is going now doesn't fill you with joy and excitement, or at a push even contentment.

You get to decide what the outcome is; I'll just help you work out what that might be, and how best to get there, all while being uniquely you. And I'll help you do this by using both my own life experience and learnings and the stories of thousands of women who have been on this journey with me.

Finally, before this chapter draws to a close, I want to explain one of the key parts of this book - a series of exercises I mentioned a little earlier which I have called "Check & Challenge".

These will be the real deciding factor as to whether this book will be a good return on investment or not; whether you decide to be in action or stay in a world of inertia and apathy.

What is Check & Challenge?

Who remembers the American Rapper Ice Cube's 1992 track "Check yourself before you Wreck Yourself"?

No?

Just me?

I spent my teenage years in the East End of London in the 1990s. My friends at school were predominantly black girls and our drug of choice was Hip Hop with an occasional splash of R&B. In many ways that genre of music is still very much a part of me, even if it does look a bit weird for a 40-year-old white woman to be bussing out the lyrics of Nas, and Public Enemy and doing the Running Man.

(My editor had no idea who these artists were or what the word "bussing" meant, which goes to show my cultural references are rather strange sometimes.)

But anyhow, what is Check & Challenge?

As women, we often have little time to sit back and reflect on our own lives. We often go through life unchallenged by others either, well positively unchallenged. What I mean by his is we tend to spend most of our time around people who think we are wonderful, or people can't wait to tell us how crap we are, often because that kind of feedback serves their own needs. Rarely do we have people in our lives who have the time, or inclination to support us in our personal development without a vested interest.

Throughout this book I wanted to gift women with the opportunity to do both of these things.

The checks and challenge prompts in this book are designed to help you check out how you feel, what you think, where you are on a particular issue or topic, and then challenge yourself to think BIGGER, to try something new, to take action towards your goals.

Without Check & Challenge, this book would just be a collection of my personal stories, with some tips and ideas for how to implement them in your life. But the Check & Challenge prompts get you to stop and take action. If you commit to spending some time really working through these, I promise you there will be big changes in the way you think, feel and behave when in comes to Living Bigger.

But you must get out of your own way, and take responsibility for your progress.

There are four ways to engage with the Check & Challenge prompts, each with a differing value attached. You get to decide how deep you want to go with each.

1. **Think** things through, spend as much or as little time considering your views, your position, your thoughts... Often there is no right or wrong answer, this is simply about tuning into yourself.

2. **Write** your response down on paper. I swear by journaling, note-taking, blogging, or anything that helps get my thoughts out of my head and into some kind of order. I love reading these back at a later date and seeing how far I have come. Use the white spaces in this book...or use a journal.

3. **Share,** now this is where it starts to get juicy. Share your findings with your friends and family, or more widely via social media. When you say things out loud and hear other people respond to your thoughts, you start to really embed them as your own. You get to show the world who you are. Remember to use the hashtags #iblamejulie and #livingabiggerlife so we can all follow your progress.

And finally

4. **Act.** Not everything you learn about yourself you are going to like. You may want to make some changes. You may want to try some new stuff out. Being in action is where you are going to make the most progress. This doesn't have to be about BIG changes; it can be subtle tweaks or just doing more of the stuff you know works for you.

So let's give it a go.

Do as many of these challenges as you can, highlight the ones which are most powerful for you and come back to them regularly...don't be scared to scribble on the pages...although not on the kindle version that would just be stupid.

Check & Challenge 1 – Let's call you out on your own bullshit

If this were one of my coaching programmes, one of the first things I would ask the women to do is to buy a lovely new journal to write stuff down in. But I know for some this is a massive turn off, and can even stop them engaging with the programme's tasks.

There is something about committing your thoughts to paper...perhaps reminding us of school, or work that instantly makes women not want to do it.

However, if you do as I suggest and write shit down in a journal, you are more likely to buy into this process overall, plus you will have a record of what you think and how your thoughts may change while on this journey.

If writing things down in nice stationary really is not your thing (I get it, I get it), scribble it down on the back of an envelope, or put it in an Instagram post, or include it in a blog post (if you should have such a thing), or simply just think it.

The main thing is not to skip the challenges.

Remember you need to do some of the work here too. It's like the best sex - it takes at least two, or maybe more, for it to work. Yes, of course you can do it alone but it gets a bit lonely after a while, and is nowhere near as satisfying, right?

So for this first Check & Challenge, I would like you to just think about your own bullshit thoughts, and perhaps list between five and 10 of them. Some of us have more bullshit knocking around our heads than others, but if you are struggling, here are a few prompts:

- Why won't this book work for you?
- What do you hate about the author (me) already?
- Why does the process not apply to you?
- Why won't you see it through?
- Why are you focussing on the author's typos/grammar/weird way of writing rather than your own thoughts on the content?
- What is triggering you?
- What are you afraid of?
- Why is it easier to put this book down now?
- Why can't you be arsed with it?

Calling out your own bullshit is liberating. Once you spot your patterns, your negative thoughts, your unhelpful thinking, you can see beyond it to find new more useful ways of being.

My particular bullshit when it comes to reading books like this one:

- Oh, I already know that (No you don't, you smartarse, read it properly and give the author a chance to explain it fully)
- Cut to the good bits (No Julie, the context is just as important as the "How to". Don't be lazy)
- Yeah, I will come back to that exercise (You NEVER do...grab a pen and do it now)

If you are feeling particularly brave, why not share your particular brand of bullshit with your social networks or with a friend. See how it feels to call yourself out.

Check & Challenge 2 – About that journal

Are you sure you don't want to go ahead and obtain a book for the purposes of writing down things you discover on this journey? I will be referring to it throughout so you might as well play along right? If you are a stationery lover, go treat yourself to a nice one (glitters and slogans are optional) but equally any old notebook or pad will do. Make sure there is enough space to fully express yourself. You may find these notes useful as we move through the chapters in this book. Further more, other people might too (but more about that later).

One of the most common bits of feedback I get from women who don't like to journal is:

"But I don't know what to write."

Often this is because they feel like they have to get all Bridget Jones about it. We are not looking for a day-by-day account of your life. Write your journal however you like. Lists, bullet points, diagrams, question and answers, the main thing is you commit to getting stuff out of your head and down onto paper.

It is easy to push your thoughts to the back of your head so you don't have to deal with them, but when you see them in black and white written in front of you they are hard to ignore. So be brave. Start writing in that journal.

Also, don't be afraid to write in this actual book if you are reading this in paperback version. Underline the bits you want to focus on, scribble notes in the margins, write lists in the back. It is your book, mark it as your own, use it as you need to.

Check & Challenge 3 – Grab yourself a reading/challenge buddy

For extra accountability, why not go through this process with someone you love and trust? Do the Check & Challenges together, discuss the content of the book, make a pact to stop being so negative about yourself or to perhaps stop dieting for a few weeks while you give this a go?

Buy them a copy of the bloody book if they are one of those annoying people who say "Yeah, yeah" but you know they might not take action.

If you really are keen to involve some of your friends in this process, have a quick look at the resources at the back of this book to help you host a Living a Bigger Life "Knees Up".

Or how about charting your progress online?

In 2013, I started a blog about being an overweight runner. It wasn't a business, I had no intention of starting a movement, I had no idea I would become an influencer (ooohhh that word!!)

I started that simple blog because I wanted a way of charting my progress and staying accountable.

Thank God I did, right?

Plus-size fitness in the UK has 100% moved on significantly because of that blog. Thousands of women are healthier and happier because of it, and it has inspired women all over the world to start running or to move up to marathon distance.

I can't take all of the credit for that because over time, this tribe of women have shared the ethos of the blog to a wider audience. I simply couldn't have done it without them.

So I am relying on you (YES YOU) to take the words of this book off the pages and into the real world. The more we talk about the concepts and ideas, the more they are embedded into life and the more these new practices become the norm.

We need to build on this movement, so that it really embeds itself into our psyche.

This is where the internet can be our friend, where we can use our social networks and social circles to our advantage. For instance, if writing is not your thing, set up an Instagram account or micro blog via Twitter. If you have never used these before, I encourage you to give it a go, you might like it. You might find it therapeutic. You might build something to be proud of, just like I have.

This book is just the beginning: the instigator, the motivator, the tool for you to use to help you understand what it is you want and what is holding you back.

It is a calling card for your future life. But the real fun starts the moment we start sharing with the world what we are up to.

Check & Challenge 4 – Chart your progress online

My social media channel of choice at the moment for this is Instagram. I like the way that not only can you document your life through pictures but you can also curate your feed of other awesome people to enable you to see the world you want to see. If you are worried about everyone seeing your business, you also get to decide whether your account is visible or not to the rest of the world.

But Facebook, Twitter, YouTube, Pinterest and Blogging can all work for this too.

I talk throughout the book about the importance of women being more visible in their lives but for now have a little look on Instagram at the #iBlameJulie or #LivingaBiggerLife hashtags to see what some of the women in my community have already started working on.

And if it feels right, start posting yourself...maybe just about the fact you are starting this process.

Right?

We ready to move on?

Great.

Let's do this.

What Does LIVING BIGGER Even Look Like?

If I died tomorrow, would it all have been worth it?

When I was about eight-years-old, we moved from our small (and oh so safe) family home in East Ham. I can barely remember now how that old house looked, but at the time it was the only place I had ever lived. It was where my friends lived, near to where I went to school, where I had learned to ride a bike, and where I had just recently been allowed to walk up to the newsagent alone... It was home.

Even though the move was just a couple of miles away from our original house, it felt like everything was changing, and it was.

We moved into a MASSIVE five-bedroom house a few minutes walk away from the West Ham United Football club grounds at Upton Park. This was to accommodate our growing family: mum, dad, and their six kids who were all under the age of ten. Oh, and Smartie, our much-loved ginger cat.

The house was huge. I even had my own room, although furniture was a bit sparse when I look back.

There were places to hide in that house where you wouldn't be found for days. With an attic and a cellar, two conservatories, two gardens, a side alley (with a coal shoot), fitted wardrobes, bay windows leading out onto the roof, it was a house crying out for games of hide and seek, or the game which we invented called "Dark Creepers" which was literally just hide and seek but with the lights off and the curtains pulled.

Why I am I telling you all of this?

Because prior to moving to that big old (but new to me) house, I don't really remember ever being unhappy as a child. Or feeling alone. Now it's mad, because with five siblings to annoy and a street full of kids to knock about with, it is seemingly impossible to be lonely. But at times at this new (old) house, I was.

Don't get me wrong, I have some real fond memories of the years we lived in that house, but our time in Central Park Road also symbolised the upheaval that was my dad leaving, my parents' divorce, and us having to move a few years later when the house got repossessed. Moving up to BIG school was kind of a big deal too (how could I forget that?).

BIG CHANGES for a little person, hey?

I can clearly remember how confused I felt during that time. I was somewhere between the ages of nine and 11 - not being so much of a child that I couldn't see some of what was going on around me, but not being mature enough to fully understand its meaning.

How I longed to be bigger so that I could play a more important role in what was going on.

This was when my bad behaviour started. I got involved in playground fights at school, went through a spell of shoplifting, and even managed to almost set the house on fire once; all for a bit of attention.

I would find myself coming up with hair-brained ideas such as turning the attic room into a library and collating all of the neighbour's books in one place; or setting up shops in the front garden to get rid of all our toys we no longer wanted. When I was 10, I decided I wanted to go to stage school to pursuit my dream of being a dancer. I applied even though I wasn't really good enough, but it was the local Convent School, St. Angela's that was to be my secondary school in the end.

Those prepubescent years were all about getting noticed, by any means necessary. I just wanted to be listened to, to be seen so that I would feel significant in some way, I guess.

Writing this I know how immature and perhaps even selfish this sounds. I was one of six kids for goodness sake, and god knows the strain my mum must have been under trying to keep her head above water.

I do wonder at times if it is this attention-seeking 10-year-old that is still driving my desire to be seen and be heard in the world, and maybe even to try and help people who also feel invisible, in a way that I was simply incapable of back then, despite my desire.

What has this got to do with living bigger?

I have a fundamental belief that we are at our BIGGEST as women, not when we are young and fearless in our late teens or early twenties, or even when we reach our more self assured 40s or 50s as some might think. Instead I believe we are actually the BIGGEST and most authentic versions of ourselves around the age of 10.

Let's think about it, for most of us at 10 years of age, the stresses and strains of responsibility haven't landed on our doorstep yet. We are still very much protected by the world, there is more equality in our day-to-day life, and we tend to be fearless in our child-like naivety. Now the number 10 is neither here nor there, as it will be different for different girls, but think about it.

When girls are born there is, at least in the world I grew up, an element of letting them do what they wish, letting them dream, imagine, and play freely. Where they can float around in princess dresses or roll around the floor in mud with little consequence. Where at school they are encouraged to think broadly about career choices (because it's all a bit of a game still) and where they are told they can do anything their male counterparts can do.

But then…

There is a point in a girl's life where this shifts and she is expected to follow rules. Lady-like rules. Such as sitting with her legs together, not farting in public, having realistic views on a future career and hobbies even. Being kind and polite even when people are not kind and polite to them. Where insidiously they are encouraged to do chores, help out in a way their brothers are not. They are expected to be so many things kind, smart, helpful, grateful, brave, vulnerable, considerate, sharing, caring, and of course humble, because nobody likes a show-off.

Now I am not a psychologist, and there are probably heaps of academics that can explain this stuff better than me, but the point I am trying to make is that when I was age eight or nine I knew exactly what I wanted to be or do when I grew up. I might not have been able to verbalise it very well, but I had a fire in my belly which lit up when I did certain activities, where I felt alive, empowered…like I was being 100% me.

This for me involved reading, writing, speaking and exploring.

Obviously, there is no way that a 10-year-old girl in the early 1990s would have been able to stand her ground and talk about her aspirations to be a future leader based on those interests; remember the internet wasn't even a thing back then, and I was a loud mouth, often slightly grubby kid from a broken home, why would anyone listen to me?

Can you see why this is kind of important?

All those years ago I knew what brought me joy, I knew where my strengths were, I knew what my path to success was, but I wasn't encouraged or supported to explore that fully. Now anyone who believes in the law of attraction or the idea that what is meant for you will find you eventually might say,

"Well you got there in the end."

But what if I am one of the lucky ones? What if I hadn't have got there in the end?

Do you know what my careers teacher suggested I did when I left school? Train to be a nursery nurse. Now I can tell you as the parent of a vibrant but oh so challenging five-year-old, I couldn't think of anything I would hate more.

But this is not just about career paths.

Living Bigger is one of those tenuous concepts that is fundamentally about who you are at your core, like having the space to be your true self, to reach your full potential, before any of life's many layers of conditioning get in the way, before we let other people's needs come before ours, before we kind of give up a little on our dreams.

Check & Challenge 5 – What did you want to be and why as a 10-year-old?

Now I am going to be frank with you, I never considered myself a feminist until recently.

In honesty, I couldn't really be arsed to look into what it really meant, and I was too busy convincing myself everything was pretty equal anyway. I was blinkered. That was until it started impacting on me.

Through my 20s and early 30s, I saw snippets of inequality, and there were things that happened to me where I thought, "That's not right" or where I was absolutely disadvantaged or looked over for opportunities because I was a woman.

It was only when I started working so closely with other women on achieving their goals, it was only when I took a long hard look at my own story, and those of the women in my family who came before me that I realised that things were not fair, and that I wasn't going to be quiet about it any longer.

There was absolutely a shift in my attitude after becoming a mum, especially a mother of a daughter. I now had this huge responsibility not only to be the best role model I could be, but to try and make the world she is growing up to a slightly more tolerable place to exist.

I look at my energetic five-year-old daughter, Rose, as she quite literally cartwheels through life, excited by slime, eager to learn how everything works and wanting to be a YouTube star (I know, I know), I see so much of myself in her and I try not to be triggered by my own stories about how girls should or should not behave if they want to do well in life.

I look back at my young self and try to remember the things which brought me joy, that made sense in my little head, that were oh so important to me, and think about which of these I could bring back, or let feature more in my 40-year-old life.

Check & Challenge 6 – Which (if any) of your 10-year-old qualities, hobbies, interests do you still have?

I sometimes think I am a bit like Peter Pan, like I don't want to grow up. I want to play by my own rules. When I recently turned 40, it was a bit of a shock. How on earth had I been alive for four decades? How come I didn't feel like an adult yet? How come life isn't really how I pictured it would be by this age?

I know as women we have responsibilities and we do kind of have to grow up and do adult stuff such as pay bills, get smear tests and be nice to people (within reason). However, I do think that for many of us, we have used this process of growing up as a bit of an excuse to not fully live our lives.

I know I got trapped in this in my late-30s, desperate to find a partner, in a rush to get on the property ladder, worried that I was running out of time to have kids. I started to do things which I felt were expected of me, that showed I was to be taken seriously, chasing that ever sought-after feeling of "having it all".

I couldn't keep up though.

I wasn't really being true to myself. I was making big important decisions based on ego and the fear of judgement, and inevitably it made me ill.

There I was mid-30s, living with my fiancé, a high-profile "worthy" job with a great salary, regular holidays, a brilliant social life, and everything to play for. But looking back now, I still think I was playing at life. I wasn't really being very strategic, I was just doing the bare minimum to appear like my life was great when really I wasn't very happy at all.

Things changed pretty quickly though.

I sabotaged my relationship (he wasn't right for me anyway), I lost my job (redundancy number two), I bought my first home (completely over stretching myself) and then I got completely knocked sideways by a horrific bout of depression, followed by months of Chronic Fatigue Syndrome, topped off with some pretty out-of-control drinking and partying.

Nothing was working for me.

Nothing.

I felt like I had nothing to live for, which was ludicrous because I was highly skilled, young, relatively healthy, confident, and had lots going for me.

But I had no purpose.

I think that was the biggest problem. I had no direction at all.

This was compounded by my dwindling self-esteem and low body-confidence as my weight rocketed due to emotional eating and almost no exercise.

This was the height of my yoyo dieting, I could go from a size 22 to a size 16 in a matter of months and then right back up again.

The worst thing was, even when I did get close to my goal weight I didn't feel any happier. The other areas of my life didn't automatically improve. I wasn't working on myself because I didn't understand who my self was.

That would come much later, and after many more dieting attempts.

So what is Living Bigger?

I believe for women when it comes to living a fulfilling, balanced life there are three key concepts that you need to be mindful of. Three guiding principles to help keep your life on track so you don't fall over, much like a stool needs at least three legs to stay upright.

- Health
- Wealth
- Happiness

However, if the stool was to be completely stable, and to allow for any of the others having a temporary blip, I would say the fourth pillar would be one around finding purpose. However, I feel this one is a little more fluid as it can change throughout our life. We don't always need to be driven by something in particular, sometimes we just need to be.

When women are finding the time, energy and headspace to look after these core areas of health, wealth and happiness, chances are they will feel it within their self that their life is bigger - no matter what size jeans they are wearing.

Later in the book I will go into much more details about these concepts, with specific ideas for how to keep on top of them, but for now I'd like you to have a think about how your life stands at the moment in terms of those things.

Check & Challenge 7 – Give yourself a Health, Wealth & Happiness MOT

So ladies, how often do you get yourself checked out? And no I am not talking about your smear test, or one of those health checks where, let's face it, we are simply giving our healthcare professionals a chance to tell us to lose some weight.

No seriously?

When is the last time you were given a once over? Not only in terms of your physical health, but across all areas of your life?

Never? Now why doesn't that surprise me?

If you're a motor car owner in the UK, you will know that every 12 months you have to take your vehicle in for an MOT (A Ministry of Transport) test which involves dozens of checks on your car, ranging from the brakes and fuel system to lights, mirrors, seatbelts, windscreen wipers and exhaust system.

But how often do you give yourself a full body, mind and soul MOT?

My Health, Wealth & Happiness MOT Assessment is a simple way of reviewing how you are feeling at any given point and it has helped hundreds of women to understand in quite a simple way where they currently are, and what areas of their life may need some attention.

The great thing about this assessment (other than it being 100% FREE) is that it doesn't have to be done at the start of the year, it can be done whenever you feel the need - perhaps when you are feeling most stuck, or most motivated to make a change. Ideally, you would do this at least annually, to check on progress, but there is no reason why you can't do it more frequently.

The downloadable workbook document reviews nine key areas across the health, wealth and happiness themes, which form the basis of a steady and stable well-functioning life.

You can find this FREE tool on my website **http://www.juliecreffield.com/health-and-happiness-mot/**

What have you got to lose?

Check & Challenge 8 – Review & Assess your Life from a Living BIGGER perspective

After reviewing your life via the Health & Happiness MOT, have a think or journal about the areas in your life where you believe you are not living big enough, why this might be and any immediate actions you could take to rectify this.

Who gets to define what playing BIG looks like?

Now this is a question I get a lot at the start of my Living a Bigger Life group coaching programme, and it is very telling. Because this is not about *playing* bigger. There ain't nobody playing here.

A word about the idea of playing BIG.

Somehow the phrases "playing big" and "playing small" have entered our vocabulary, and embedded themselves in the female arena, in a way you simply never hear them spoke of when it come to our male counterparts.

Often when we talk about women playing small, or playing big it is in terms of the work place, possibly in reference to gender inequality and the pay gap. With talk of glass ceilings and positive discrimination and quotas.

But rarely is it spoke about more holistically.

Cheryl Sandburg, chief finance officer of Facebook and author of the book, "Lean In" made a fantastic start in highlighting some of these issues, and making the world more aware. However, it was very much suited to women in a corporate setting, and not all women's lives look like that any more.

I want to start a conversation about all women, where we can review and make changes no matter what our lifestyle, working patterns, family set-up, dress size, race, income level and any other kind of box-ticking descriptor you can find.

A tool for ALL WOMEN.

One which can take just a few seconds to review, and adjust our thinking, behaviours or actions accordingly.

When I first started thinking about this concept of Living Bigger, I realised that because it was such a personal thing, it would be really challenging to be able to measure it, even for myself, let alone for my clients.

But isn't that how it feels when measuring health and happiness too?

They are intangible.

There is no scale.

It's just a feeling.

Sitting at home in front of the TV on a Friday night could make one woman the happiest ever because she rarely gets the chance to just relax, and this is exactly what her body needs, this is her living BIG. Yet for another woman doing this night after night because she has nobody to hang out with and is coping with loneliness and self-doubt, this could feel completely different.

This activity could be considered living big or living small…or we could just not read into it at all, it could just be a woman sitting on the sofa. And while talking about sofas, in the context of health and fitness, I hate the fact the sofa gets blamed so much.

Sensationalist newspaper headlines and phrases such as:

Couch potato lifestyle to blame for rising obesity levels
I might be slow but at least I am lapping everyone on the sofa
Lazing on sofa for as little as two weeks leads to decline in health

Let us not shame women into not being able to relax after a hard day, please? We get to decided how much is too much, and if we need to have a sofa day we should be able to without the fear of judgement.

And actually when it comes to judgement, this is not a tool to start comparing our lives to those of other women. This is not another tool to beat women over the head with – just because I'm living bigger in an area of my life, it doesn't give me permission to assume someone else isn't because they have made different choices.

This is all about choice.

Choice and perception.

How do we even start to define the scale of our life if it is different for different women?

Funny you should ask that.

I knew I would have to come up with some kind of tool though to help women quantify their own habits, behaviours and feelings to make sense of the Living Bigger concept, and that it would have to be completely devoid of judgement.

I don't know about you, but I am done with being judged by other people. In fact, I am done with judging myself unnecessarily too.

This tool would simply be about reviewing my thoughts and feelings with a view to making small or maybe even significant adjustments, devoid of the normal "Fuck man I need to do something about this ASAP" kind of response that so many of us are prone to.

So, here it is.

Introducing the "How Big Are You Living" Quadrant Tool......

You can download a copy of this from **www.juliecreffield.com/LBLresources**

I suggest you do, and print it out and stick it somewhere you will see it multiple times a day. I have one on my desk, in my diary, in my car, on my fridge...you get the idea.

The Living Bigger Quadrant Tool

This diagram is a simple way for you to get into the habit of assessing how you are turning up in the world. There is no science behind it, instead, this will be based on your gut instinct and your sense of how you want to live your life.

There are two axes to consider **Awareness** and **Expansive Living**, which help you to understand the extent to which you are engaging fully in all of the joys, challenges, and experiences that this life throws at us.

The easiest way to use this diagram is to ask yourself: "Am I Living Big or Small here?" and "Am I or was I conscious of this or not?" These two questions will help you work out which zone you are functioning from.

There are two axes:

1. **The Awareness Axis** is all about how conscious you are of your actions, behaviours, and environment.

And

2. **The Expansive Living Axis** is all about scale, whether something is being done in a small, understated way (or not at all) or in a larger bolder capacity.

These two axes create four clear zones. These zones can give you an idea as to the level you are currently functioning at.

The four quadrants are

1. **Growth Zone**
2. **Woeful Zone**
3. **Credit Zone**
4. **Joyful Zone**

It is important though not to judge yourself too harshly, and to see this tool as exactly that a tool, to enable you to be more aware and to act as a prompt to make some changes if you should want to.

51

Let me talk a bit further about the zones.

The Joyful Zone
This is where you want to be, living your fullest life and being in a place where you absolutely know you are so you can be grateful for it and invite even more of this into your world

This zone in my mind is coloured green as a reminder that it's all systems go. This way of life is around being "in flow". You will know when you are there because it will feel epic either in an adrenaline-fuelled "Fuck yeah I just nailed that" kind of way, or with a calmer "yep I know, I'm a goddess" kinda vibe.

I was 100% in the Joyful Zone after the first few minutes of my TEDx, and I am normally here after the first mile or so of the marathons I have run, or while flying first class back from a conference in Orlando and feeling like I 100% belonged.

As with all of this stuff though, you get to decide what feels joyful.

Woeful Zone
This is the complete opposite to the Joyful Zone...you might like to think of it as the red zone. We really don't want to be in here if possible because it is the zone where we make the least progress, and sadly where our health and happiness suffers most. We are functioning on a small scale, not showing our best self and the sad thing is we don't even know it. Sometimes we find ourselves here because we have our blinkers on, actively avoiding the issue. The easiest way to avoid this zone is to practice regular self-awareness activities.

The two key times in my life where I feel I was in the woeful zone was during my 30s when I was using partying as a way of hiding my sadness and unfulfilled life, and also shortly after my daughter was born when I absolutely lost who I was as a person.

Next, this is where it gets interesting.

Credit Zone
Here you are living big (or maybe even playing big) but you are just not aware of it yet. This is where you need to start giving yourself more credit for the places that you do consistently show up. Where you are shit hot at whatever it is you are doing. With a bit of awareness and gratitude, it is easy to jump up to the joyful zone and start applying this to other areas of your life.

Lots of women have talents and skills that they hide from the world and if they had more self-awareness and a bit more visibility, they would have a much greater sense of purpose.

For me, I never really valued my writing talents. I am not the best at grammar or spelling (my school experience wasn't that great) but I do have a flair for writing from the heart and being able to inspire women with my words.

I could probably give myself more credit for my sporting achievements. I am not a great runner in terms of speed, but I am great in terms of my determination and endurance.

Finally, this is the zone which I think has the most potential when it comes to shifting things around and bringing you closer to your goals...

And finally...

Growth Zone

This is a great place to be for learning about yourself. You may be living smaller than you would like to but you know you are and are actively working towards addressing that. In the growth zone, you are vulnerable but there is also strength in that. You are facing your fears, learning new skills, changing your attitude and people around you start to notice. It is also worth noting that in the growth zone you may be procrastinating a bit; you know you are not working to your full potential but you are self-sabotaging by not making any changes.

Check & Challenge 9 – Which Zone can you be found in?

Can you find areas of your life which you can already see fitting into this quadrant? Make a list of three or four in each category, if you can.

How to use this tool in your day-to-day life?

I have this quadrant printed up and stuck all around me. On my computer screen, in my home office, in my work diary, on a mirror in my bedroom... I use it as a prompt to remind me to be more aware.

- I use it to question my actions when I am procrastinating
- I use it when making challenging decisions
- I use it when I am planning
- I use it when something has gone a bit tits up
- I use it when I am stuck

The quadrant can work nicely alongside the themes of the Health, Wealth & Happiness MOT, where you literally ask yourself,

"Where am I in the Living a Bigger Life quadrant when it comes to my health, or my happiness, or my relationships?"

Or even more detailed than that:

"Where am I in that quadrant when it comes to my running or how I am approaching my job?"

"How did I do this evening when my friend made that slightly weird comment?"

"What was I doing when I yelled at my five-year-old excessively tonight?"

One of my coaching clients used this tool at the start of one of my programmes and the results of it inevitably led her to a complete change of career and embarking on a degree course. She said,

"So I decided to fill out the quadrant using the MOT following last night's call. I've realised that my woeful zone is around my skills wealth, which is preventing me from moving on career wise. Everything else was in the other three zones even if just by a little bit!"

This tool gave her the clarity to see the area she needed to focus on most, without any sense of negative judgement, which we are often so quick to do.

Check and Challenge 10 – 10 areas for review

Take a look at the quadrant in response to the following 10 areas of your life and see what comes up? Feel free to add any categories you feel are missing, or remove those not relevant.

- Health
- Wealth
- Happiness
- Spirituality
- Skills
- Work/Business
- Parenting
- Love
- Friendship
- Community

This tool doesn't necessarily give you the answers to why you might not be living your life to the fullest, but it does raise awareness and that is an important preliminary step. It can also help you to spot trends and patterns too.

Over the years, I have worked with so many women who come to me feeling like they are not living the life they want, but who can't pin down what the problem is. It doesn't take much to get them uncovering what the issue is, often all it takes is encouraging them to sit down and actually think about it for a bit.

In many cases, these women have found themselves in their current situation over a long period of time. With years of putting others first, shutting out their own thoughts and feelings, literally putting their own needs on hold. The average age of my clients is around 45 or 46, and for many of them joining one of my programmes represents the first time that they have had the space to consider themselves.

Also many of my women have purposefully disassociated themselves from their sense of self, often because they don't value or even really like themselves that much.

Having lived in a bigger body for all of my adult life, I used to think these issues were unique to us FAT women, but I have since realised that women of all shapes and sizes have feelings of "unworthiness", "self loathing" and "imposter syndrome".

However, lots of women find me through my work as a plus-size fitness blogger, meaning I work a lot with overweight women, and I think it is worth talking about why the strategies in this book are so important for larger women.

A word about why living small is problematic for FAT women

Let's face it, there are certain things in the world where it is generally accepted that bigger is better.

- Cream cakes
- Diamond rings
- Cars
- Willies
- Boobs
- Bank balances

(Although reading that list back, it's all still quite subjective)

But there is no denying it, when it comes to women it is quite clear that we are supposed to be small. Small in stature, small in opinion, small in ambition. Well, at least that's how it used to be before we decided this was just a teeny, tiny bit unfair.

Now I am not really an expert in feminism or the women's movement, but what I do know is that despite the progress which has been made over the past few centuries, many of the things which keep women down or at least put as at a disadvantage, are still very much in place...

- Corsets and shapewear
- Unequal pay
- Male-dominated industries
- Period poverty
- The share of parenting and caring responsibilities

But the thing which gets my goat the most is the unrealistic expectations which are put on women when it comes to their appearance and what they look like. Sure, some women are enjoying a more equal world, but we still live in a world full of judgement and discrimination where people do not always look upon overweight women favourably.

Whether we like it or not there is, whether conscious or unconscious, a belief that overweight women are stupid, lazy, gluttonous, have no control, don't love themselves, are irresponsible.

I remember at the screening of my TEDx during the Q&A, a male from the audience tried to imply that plus-size women are not discriminated against. First, how the hell would he know? Often this kind of behaviour goes completely under the radar meaning if you are not fat, you wouldn't see it.

But also, he said, as a fly away comment:

"I've dated plus-size women."

I wanted to say in response,

"Do you want a fucking medal?"

Of course I didn't, but I often wondered if I should have.

Standing up to inappropriate comments about your size, or even just the way you look is not easy. I wish I had wonderful come backs all the time, but often I don't and I spend the next few hours stewing over what I should have said in response. Which in itself can be cathartic, and if nothing else makes for great stand-up comedy material.

True story coming up...

I was once cycling along the road minding my own business when a van pulled up alongside me with two blokes in it, one of whom shouted out: "I wish my face was that saddle". I know, I know it is a bit crass and I did wonder about including this story in this book, but bear with me.

It took me a few seconds to work out what he had even said, and then the shock left me speechless as they sped off laughing to themselves. I was gutted that I didn't have something to say back to them instantly, and it made me feel like a right idiot.

Later that evening, I came up with a number of responses for if ever I should get the same comment, and years later I incorporated them into a stand-up routine, which went a bit like this:

"It's hard being a plus-size athlete because we do get heckled. Once I was cycling along the road minding my own business when a van pulled up and a bloke shouted: "I wish my face was that saddle". To which I responded, "Really??? Cos I'm on my period". I bet that left him with a bitter taste in his mouth - and a bit red-faced."

Equally as crass, but that line won me a best newcomers place in a local comedy night competition, and a roar of laughter when I did a short impromptu gig at a comedy night in Cape Town, South Africa. Some jokes are universal it seems.

I still haven't come up with a witty response for when my former father-in-law says: "You're looking fat these days" but I am working on it.

The point is, often we do get the same or similar comments which hurt or annoy or anger us, and we are not always best equipped or prepared to respond how we would like. I know it's not our job to educate idiots about how to interact in life, but sadly we have to sometimes, and if enough of us do it I believe things such as cat calling and internet trolling about women's appearances will lesson over time.

Check & Challenge 11 – Dealing with inappropriate comments

Make a list of all the inappropriate comments you have had about your body or the way you look. How they made you feel. Why you allowed them to make you feel that way. And an appropriate response. Next step is to trial using them.

One of my favourite uses of this is with the rather unfortunate:

"Oh you're pregnant" or "When's the baby due" from a complete stranger.

I now say, "I'm not pregnant, I'm just fat" and then leave a "pregnant gap" while smiling at them.

And when they apologise sounding completely mortified, I then say:

"A useful reminder not to comment on people's appearance, hey?"

I try to do this without spite, or anger, or as if it had hit a nerve, so that they don't ever feel the need to make assumptions about a stranger's body again.

Wouldn't it be great if people just didn't comment on your body? Even when people think they are being nice with "Oh, you've lost weight?" I would rather people just didn't. I know often what people are trying to do is pay you a compliment, but weight loss at any cost shouldn't be celebrated in my view.

Do we celebrate when someone loses weight because of an illness? Or make an issue if someone has gained weight in similar circumstances? No that would be super inappropriate, wouldn't it?

But body shaming still remains a reasonably acceptable form of discrimination, the last available butt of a joke it seems, and women are at the forefront of that, you only have to see the cover of women's magazines shaming the latest celebrity to gain weight to see how unacceptable it is to be visible and fat.

I am sure men get it at all under the guise of banter, but somehow it doesn't feel like it's the same thing.

When it comes to representation, you tell me the last time you saw a larger-than-average women held up as an example of success. I think Opera Winfrey was the only one I could think of growing up, along with Dawn French maybe. However, in the latter case, I am not sure that comediennes count, because in many ways we were laughing at their fatness, or if not laughing directly at it, most definitely laughing along with it.

Hollywood and the occasional reality TV show have churned out some overweight celebrities who we have taken to our hearts, but it is still not a level playing field.

We were fed very clear messages as children that being fat was not acceptable, and most definitely wouldn't help us live a happy life.

"Watch what she eats, Jan, you don't want her to get BIG."
"You won't get a boyfriend if you get too FAT."
"Oh don't worry, it's just puppy fat, you will grow out of it."

Two thirds of 11- to 18-year-olds would rather be stupid than fat, and get this, 50% would rather be run over by a truck, according to a study by the Healthy Lifestyles Research Center at Arizona State University.

Wow.

So it's hardly any wonder that so many women report going on their first diet at the age of 12 or 13, whether they were considered overweight or not, and after 30 years of yoyo dieting and self-hatred are now at a complete lost for what to try next.

This is a problem throughout the western world, because let's remember larger bodies are seen as a display of wealth or fertility in some other cultures. The fear of being fat is at an all-time high and not because of any suggested health implications but because of what it means socially, and how you might be treated or judged unfairly in a bigger body.

We will be exploring a lot of this later in the book, but for now I just wanted to hit you with the headlines, many of which I included in my TEDx talk, because people need to know about this stuff, even if they have no experience of being overweight themselves.

Did you know in the UK, two million fewer women than men play sport because of the fear of judgment? The fear of looking stupid, the fear of not being good enough, the fear of being laughed at...

For overweight women, these fears are often multiplied. And this fear of judgment is not just limited to sports with these feelings also surfacing during all kinds of everyday activities, such as showing up at the supermarket, at the school gate, in night clubs, at conferences...

Even after running hundreds of races all over the world, including half-marathons, marathons, Tough Mudders and a 40-mile ultra-marathon, I still often feel like I am being judged. When I tell people I run marathons, I suspect they don't believe me, or they imagine I must have a terrible diet.

I don't think we realise how crippling fear can be for some women. Over the years, I have heard tales of women running on treadmills in garden sheds because they are too scared to run in public; women who run in secret and hide all their kit, in case their children or husbands laugh or ridicule them; women who sign up for races, train for them and then repeatedly don't show up on the day because they can't face the prospect of coming last or being photographed.

If millions of women around the world don't play sport because of the fear of judgment what else are they not doing in life because of this fear?

I once had a client in my online running club from the Himalayas, she ran under the cover of darkness, because sport for women of her age (and size) was frowned upon by the other people in her community.

Shocking hey?

Check & Challenge 12 – What has fear held you back from doing?

Can you think of a time where you let your fear stop you from doing something you really wanted to do? Make a list in your journal of things you would have loved to do that would have improved your health, wealth or happiness. We will be coming back to these in a later chapter, when we start making plans for our BIGGER Life.

Things I wished I had done in my late teens and early 20s but didn't because of the fear of judgment?

- Be a holiday rep for a season
- Flat share
- Take up rugby
- Continue dancing
- Take part in Notting Hill Carnival
- Go to music festivals
- Pursue acting as a career

Having lived in a larger body for all of my adult life, I used to think the way I felt was unique to me being the size I am. It is not. I used to think only overweight women hated their bodies, battled with food addictions, felt self conscious about how they looked. This is not the case, and the more I speak to women of all shapes and sizes, I realise that being overweight is not a requirement for feeling this way.

I do find it pretty ironic though that larger women who literally take up more physical space on this planet often try to minimize themselves (both in terms of how they position their bodies, and how they show up in life) and shrink in order to make themselves more palatable to the world.

There is an internet meme doing the rounds which says,

I am smart, talented and beautiful, so to be slim too would just be unfair.

Although I hate it because it pitches slim and larger people against each other and still implies slimness is the goal, I do wonder whether for some of us we do fear being too much in this world, and believe that age old adage that as women you can't have it all.

This book is not just about overcoming your fears, insecurities and hang-ups as a larger lady. It's about looking at these things no matter what size you happen to be. But I must reference the role that being overweight has played in being able to identify these thoughts and feelings for myself, and also highlight the role that dieting or the pressure to look a certain way has played in the lives of most women's views of themselves.

You have to be able to see the BIGGER you, to be able to work towards it

So whatever your current size, whether you are still in dieting mode or not, whether you secretly or not so secretly desire to change your body, we are about to dig deeper into what it feels like to start living bigger.

A few warnings:

You may feel resistant to some of these ideas.
You may not want to face up to some of this stuff.
You may not want to dig deep into your history.
You may not want to look to the future
You may simply be just too comfortable exactly where you are.

But let's just give it a chance, shall we?
Let us just see where we end up?
See where this journey takes us.

Remember, Living Bigger means different things to different women, depending on their values and aspirations, their life-forming stories, their current circumstances and their dreams for the future.

Only you get to define what Living Bigger looks and feels like for you

And you get to choose what areas you want to focus on as we move forward.

But just so we are all on the same page with a shared understanding, my interpretation of Living Bigger means living authentically (showing up exactly as you are) and with autonomy (freedom to choose) and striving to be the best version of yourself.

What would that look like for you?

Check & Challenge 13 – Visualising the BIGGER you

If you have been a dieter or if you have been on any kind of quest to change your appearance, you will know just how important it is to be able to visualise yourself at your goal weight or with a better wardrobe, or straighter hair, or new boobs (whatever it is for you). But equally, you may know how difficult that visualisation piece can be.

Being able to visualise your life exponentially different from how it is now can be super hard. But in order to move towards the life we want, we must know where we are heading and the power of visualisation is incredibly important.

How can we know what we don't want, if we can't see what we do want?

It's like having an arsehole boyfriend that you don't know is an arsehole until you see how other men treat their women, and you see what you are missing.

Or thinking that a twin-tub washer is the nuts until you realise there is a machine that washes AND dries your clothes all in one go, without you having to do anything but load and unload when its done.

Keep your eyes peeled for a new and improved option and then you can work out what you want for the future right?

Take some time to write in your journal what a BIGGER you might look like.

- How do you spend your time?
- What activities do you do?
- How do you show up?
- How do you take care of yourself?
- What do you no longer do?
- What gets you out of bed in the morning?
- What brings you joy?
- How do others see you?
- How do you see yourself?

Check & Challenge 14 – Dare to dream

Do you dream?

I'm not really talking about the stuff that happens when you are asleep, I am talking about the activity of imagining or playing out scenarios when you are wide awake or on the periphery of sleep.

I do.

I always have.

I've dreamed about meeting my ideal man, buying a new house, winning the lottery (who hasn't?) and scaling my business.

The great thing about day dreaming is that you get to direct the stories, the characters, the narrative and the details, and if you change your mind or want something different, you can do it all over again the way you want it?

But why bother?

What goes on in your own mind is your business and your business alone. How often have you expressed a dream only to have it knocked down or laughed at by someone else?

Being able to create and curate new worlds and exciting lives in the safety of your own mind allows you to play, to imagine, to try things on for size. It is fun, it is exciting, but it also helps you to really hone in on what it is you want for yourself.

Have some fun each night before you go to sleep creating and directing scenarios that involve you living your bigger life, really focus on letting things play out exactly how you want them and remember how it feels being that person.

Notice any resistance you have to any of the details, such as:

"I walk into the room wearing a wonderful red dress (oh shit, I can't wear red because my mum always said it wasn't my colour.)"

Or

"And then I buy my dream car (but what would my husband say about spending so much money?)"

If you like, you can transfer some of these to your journal, but you don't have to. The point of day dreaming is literally to visualise a life you want for yourself and to evoke the feelings so that when things start happening in real life it doesn't feel completely alien, and you can identify that they are things you do indeed want.

We will be covering how to dream big and how to get away from the "how will I?" to the "why must I?" a little later in the book.

Before we do that I have to just make the case again for why we should consider giving up diets. Namely, that we are going to be busy doing new and exciting things. We won't have time to be counting calories, hating on ourselves, or standing in line to be weighed in a cold, community centre.

Ready to start working toward a BIGGER life yet?

Why Diets Just Don't Work

"I would join your anti diet programme, but that would mean cancelling my slimming club membership and I've been going for 20 years"

Excuse me why I take a bit of a deep breath.

This might get messy.

Right.

I'm going in.

Have you ever been with a group of women having a grand old time and then someone mentions having put weight on, what their latest way of eating is, or how much weight they need to lose before a special occasion coming up, and then before you know it all hell breaks loose and you find yourself caught up in a full blown dieting chow down?

Even if at your core you believe that diets don't work, and are a firm believe in body positivity?

Even if you want to scream at your size-10 friend: "If you are FAT what the hell does that make me?"

Even if there are like a billion and one other things you would rather spend time discussing with your smart, funny, interesting pals than dieting?

But still the conversation goes on, until everyone feels just about the right level of shit about themselves and someone finally changes the topic.

Sadly, we are conditioned to talk about diets, about being smaller, about being better as women from a very very young age. In many ways its like a passage into adulthood. It brings us all together somehow with shared goals, shared struggle, a shared experience.

Because we all know that women who love their bodies EXACTLY as they are just weird right? Maybe that's why we follow them on Instagram and watch them on reality TV, for the spectacles that they are...

Ever wondered what women would talk about if they couldn't talk about diets, dieting, how big their bum had got, how they can't wear stripes or what they wouldn't do to fit into those white Levi jeans they wore aged 16? (Remind me to tell you the story of my white jeans later?)

I went on my first official diet around the age of 13, I think it was during the summer as I was off school and mum was doing Slim Fast again, and this time we were going to do it together. A little later I also attended Weight Watchers, but I couldn't tell you exactly how old I was as the memories are quite blurred. Chances are my mum would deny this even happened.

Now just a note about my mum.

I love her.

This book is not intended to throw her under the bus in any way. She did the best she could with what she had available to her, and I am grateful for the person she has helped me to become, no matter how painful at times the journey has been.

I don't for a minute think my mum meant to teach me the things she did about dieting or hating her/my body, but sadly she was ill-equipped to pass on anything different from the messages she got herself growing up. Remember there were no body positive memes anywhere to be found in her teenage years…and very little useful information about healthy lifestyles or looking after your mental health either.

Just needed to make that clear.

As we start to explore our personal stories, our journeys towards becoming the women we are today, this is not an opportunity to start blaming and shaming those in our stories. Holding onto resentment, making them responsible for any heartache or hardship we feel now will not help us (or them). Instead it's time to understand, accept, forgive and move the hell on. There will be more of this in Chapter 7 when we look at stories some more.

My story with dieting

Some of my earliest memories of my mum were around her total dissatisfaction with her body. It is hardly any wonder as it had been through a lot over the years. She had given birth to six small people in the space of 10 years for a start, and if that wasn't enough Hodgkin's Lymphoma had stripped it of any of the remaining vitality a woman in her 30s should still have.

I can remember the aerobics in the front room, the eating of celery sticks, the squeezing into jeans while laying flat on her bed… But most importantly what I remembered was the constant conversations that went on between the adult women in my family. Who was on what diet, how much they had lost at Weight Watchers, and how certain foods were naughty but oh so nice.

Mum didn't influence me in this way out of spite. She wasn't even aware of it. In many ways it was just a sign of the times. The dieting industry was ramping up, aerobics stars such as Jane Fonda and Rosemary Connolly were rising to fame and people were buying into the idea that slimmer was better, hook line and sinker.

I thought dieting was normal. I thought all teenagers dieted with their mums because this was my normal.

My mum was not alone in this.

A couple of months ago I posted in **The Clubhouse**, my online running club's Facebook Group a question about how old members were when they went on their first diet. I was astounded by the amount of women who had been forced onto diets under the age of 18, and just how shocking some of the stories were.

Check & Challenge 15: When did you go on your first diet and why?

Have a go at writing in your journal about how it felt to embark on your first diet. If writing it out in long hand feels weird, perhaps do some kind of timeline or a flow chart. The important thing is that you get it onto paper in some kind of visual format.

When I was a young girl, every Saturday morning I would head to the local church hall (you know the ones that are always freezing in winter) for dance school. Here we would practice our routines ready for the show that we'd inevitably be putting on in the local old people's home, while our mums got a couple of hours to themselves.

One thing I remember about this time is hearing our mums discussing our changing body shapes and talking about "watching what we're eating" and "being careful that we didn't get fat" – even though none of us were destined to be professional ballerinas and were dancing for fun.
I was never a petite child, but looking back at old photos it is clear to see that I wasn't overweight. I was tall for my age though, and because of this I never really felt comfortable in my body, and would often compare myself to the more slender, smaller, petite girls.

I have a really clear memory of having a strop in C&A, aged 10, sitting in a changing room in a bikini feeling completely naked and mum refusing to buy it for me because it: "Didn't suit me", which of course I read as "Oh, I'm too fat".

Fat was the ultimate insult while I was growing up.

It was the weapon of choice at school.

Do you remember when at some time during the 80s there was a spell of "your mum is so fat..." jokes, and boys would take any chance they got to call you fat in front of everyone.

Whether you were or were not wasn't really the point - they just knew it was an insult and would make them look big in front of their friends.

If only I knew then what I know now.

That my body was fine, in fact it was more than fine.

I didn't need to go on a diet.

The food I ate was perfectly healthy.

My attitudes towards food were too.

That my body would go on to do brilliant things without it ever being skinny.

Let's talk about the F word

I have never shied away from using provocative language. I say what I think. I don't mince my words. I swear. I can be crass. I can be blunt and shock with my words. So it is hardly any wonder that I have built a brand around one of the most provocative words in the dictionary.

FAT

Such a simple word, but boy is it loaded.
In the past it has absolutely cut me to the core, but its funny since using it in the description of my blog it has lost all that negative power it had over me.

If someone calls me FAT now, I'm like erm yeah!!!

I've also found that for people who know me and still want to use the word to hurt me, it has stopped them in their tracks, or at least served as a tool to remind them that they probably won't get the impact they were hoping for.

I remember the first time my ex called me fat during an argument. Of course he apologised profusely afterwards, but it shone a light on how he really saw me. I will talk more about how men engage in the fat debate when it comes to women later as I don't want us to get into a gender battle so early in the book.

But men and women do use the word FAT differently when using it to hurt and control others.

I use the word FAT now as a descriptor. No more. No less. It isn't a loaded word for me anymore. Although I do appreciate it isn't like this for all women, and so I am mindful not to forget how hurtful it can still be when used.

Check & Challenge 16 – How do you feel about the word FAT?

List in your journal the times the word "fat" has been used against you, how it made you feel and how it would feel if it wasn't so loaded?

I believe a really powerful way of changing the conversation about women's bodies, and the question of health and obesity is to normalise the word fat, to strip it of its negative connotations and uses as an insult. Much like we use words like tall, or dark-skinned, or blonde to describe your appearance.

In many ways, this starts with conversations we have with our kids. Children learn early which words can be used as weapons. How many times has a young boy used the term, "that's so gay" in relation to something, without really understanding the fullness of that statement?

Most of us learn that the word "fat" is a naughty, insulting word from a really young age, and it's adults who often unknowingly teach us this, be this our parents, relatives or teachers. The conversation usually goes a little bit like this,

Child: "Mummy, Mummy, that man's really FAT!!!!"
And this is usually said at the top of their voice, causing embarrassment and a sense of panic for the adult, as those around (possibly even the man himself) watch to see what is done or said in response.

Mum: "Shhhhh, don't say that sweetie".

Child: "Whhhhyyyyyy?????"

Mum: "Because it's not nice to call people FAT."

Child: "But he is FAT."

Mum: "I know...but it's still not nice."

Child: "OK, Mummy."

And then the child stores that information away in their little brain under things that are not nice to say about others along with "I'd better not get fat either as people will shout out mean things if I do" resulting in double whammy!!!

I like to think of fatness just like any other way of describing someone's appearance, a bit like the children's game of Guess Who.

Player 1 – "Does your person have red hair?"

Player 2 – No (Tap, Tap, Tap Tap). "Does your person have blue eyes?"

Player 1 – "Erm nope." (Tap, Tap, Tap Tap) "Is yours wearing a hat?"

Player 2 – "Yep."

Player 1 – "Is it Mary?"

It is hard to install this kind of beliefs in your children when the world is telling them something completely different.

What if the conversation went like this instead:

Child: "Mummy, Mummy, that man's really FAT!!!!"

Mum: "Yes he is."

Child: "Like Auntie Julie (or insert any other person, cartoon character etc.)"

Mum: "Yes, that's right."

Child: "OK."

Mum: "Some people don't like their appearance being commented on though, so next time
let's not shout things like that out so loudly, hey?"

Child: "OK Mummy."

This stuff does matter and as parents we have to be prepared to have these conversations.
A few months ago, my five-year-old daughter came back from gymnastics at school

desperate to show me her progress. She told me they had done step-ups onto a bench for 15 minutes to build strength in their legs, and I commented that her legs were looking really strong to which she replied:

"Do I look skinny?"

She is five!!!

She recently got weighed as part of the government's initiative to measure all reception age children and now she is super-aware of body size. She came home telling me the nurse told her she was healthy (although I am not sure if this did or did not happen)

She is healthy.

She eats well, regularly takes part in sport and activities outside of school, and is rarely
unwell.

However, the official letter came back saying she was overweight and gave me some rather condescending advice around diet and exercise:

"You may wish to be more physically active"

Go figure.

She tells me that being fat isn't healthy but being skinny is, and in the next breath, she's saying that it doesn't matter what size you are as long as you are healthy. Talk about mixed messages?

Every day, I have to check my language and check my behaviour around food and exercise to make sure I am not passing on any of my bad habits.

She also tells me children in her school call me FAT, to which I respond:

"YES, I am and I love my body. Remember people come in all shapes and sizes."
Yeeeeeessssshhhh, where does it end?

I want her to be a child and to go play, and learn and experience things, not be worrying about her body or mine come to think about it.

There are many mixed messages coming from all angles: be it the school nurse, magazines, social media, films, and even our own attitudes. For example, in the past, many mothers and fathers thought that teaching us that FAT was a bad thing would help us not become it, like it was a bloody disease.

The legacy of passing body issues on to our offspring is not one we can ignore. Instead of creating pressure and negativity, we should be creating a positive message – one that acknowledges that healthy bodies come in all shapes and sizes.

Check & Challenge 17 – What early messages did you get about your body growing up?

Have a think and write in your journal any comments or messages you received about your body growing up and who from. Do you find yourself repeating these to (or in front of) your own children if you have them? We will refer back to these later in the book.

While researching for my TEDx talk I started asking the women in my coaching groups what they thought? I also started a poll to find out how widespread early dieting practices were.

The results were shocking:

In the Too Fat too Run Clubhouse, **67% of women had been put on a diet by their mother before the age of 16, whereas on the Fat Girl's Guide to Running public Facebook Page, that figure was higher at 69%.**

That is shocking enough, but the stories that came with it have literally had me in tears

"Sent to school with salad in stork margarine pot at 10 years old. Looking back I wasn't even chubby, but I didn't size up to my mum's friend's daughter"

"About 11 for me and bullied by my own brother and sister for being fat!!!!!! Have been on a diet ever since."

"Being 'on a diet' has been in my vocabulary since I can remember and I was put on my first 'diet' when I was 10 just before I went to high school. I wasn't overweight, my parents monitored what I ate for health reasons. I wasn't allowed crisps, chocolate or anything with lots of fat or sugar."

"Saturday at our house was weigh day and our weights were marked on a graph stuck to the fridge."

"My mum put me on a diet aged 10 coz I was getting 'chubby'. I started my periods around the same time and I remember being so hungry I started hiding food and binging. I've yo-yo dieted ever since"

"My mum used to call me fat-related names because the doctor told her to shock me into losing weight. I'm sure that's not what he meant but it's what my mum thought him to mean"

"My mum was always talking about me being overweight even though I wasn't. I just got boobs and hips early!!!"

For many of us dieting has been such a part of our lives for such a long time that it is ingrained in the way we think and really hard to shake off.

Now you might be reading this thinking, "well, there is nothing wrong with sending your kids to school with a salad for lunch, or not allowing them sweets and chocolate." That's kind of not the point. The point is these women were aware that their parents were doing this to make them smaller. This is what damaged their self-esteem, not the healthy food.

These messages highlight how mothers (and fathers) have an important role to play in helping our children – especially our girls – to feel positive about themselves, and to remind them how wonderful they are and that their bodies or how they look does not define them as a person.

It makes me feel so angry, so sad, so helpless that millions of women all over the world spend so much of their lives focusing on food and getting to their ideal weight, when most will never achieve this. So much time, energy and money is wasted by women who believe that life will start when they have an acceptable body, and that they will only be worthy of love, happiness and success when they are no longer fat.

It is rarely acceptable to put your daughter on a diet (the only situation I can think of is if there is a medical condition that requires a special diet) and it is NEVER acceptable to comment on their body in a way that is likely to make them feel bad about themselves. This just serves to tell them that they are no good as they are and encourages them to develop unhealthy or even secretive behaviours around food. Shaming never works, it just encourages women to be more secretive.

Tweak the whole family's eating for sure, introduce more exercise for everyone…but focusing on a child's body size and explicitly trying to make them conform is just not on.

I am not a dietician nor an expert on childhood obesity but what I do know is that if you feed your kids proper foods in sensible portions most of the time, and get them involved in activities that they enjoy, then their body (you know that thing which is super clever?) will somehow manage to regulate hunger and the likes by itself.

Obviously, when they are adults they can make their own choices about lifestyle, but most of this will be informed by their experiences growing up anyway, so focus on your own behaviours rather than fixating on their thinness.

The most important thing to feed your kids though is buckets and buckets full of love, self-acceptance and confidence in their bodies because boy oh boy are they going to need it as they journey into adulthood.

Especially girls.

I still can't get over the fact that the average woman in the UK spends 31 years on a diet...we are not talking the average FAT woman, this statistic was from a general Ipso Mori survey in 2006 about attitudes to food, so we are talking the average woman.

31 bloody years!!!

That's a long time to be caught up in the bubble of hope/despair, restriction/binge. good/bad, success/failure, believing that food is the enemy and that life will get better if only you could stick to the diet this time.

The report, which was commissioned by the cheese company that make Laughing Cow Light (oh the irony), revealed that British women spend on average six months a year counting calories, and a fifth of the women surveyed are on a permanent diet.

It is exhausting.

In the past, I have always had this nagging fear that when I talk publically about food or the fact I "don't diet" that people who have never battled with their weight will be rolling their eyes and already imagining what this means for an already overweight person.

Because let's face it, overweight people are lazy, gluttonous and stupid, right?

I've been called out on Twitter after appearing in the media: "Oh great, a fat woman telling us what to eat"

When I actually wasn't telling people what to eat, only sharing my own experiences.

Being told via email: "You are encouraging obesity by stating you are healthy when you are not"

And being repeatedly asked: "Do you have to eat loads/stay fat to stay on brand?"

So, yes it is time for me to start speaking out to challenge this level of ignorance.

In my experience of working with overweight women, the amount of time, money, energy and effort that overweight women put into dieting and eating well in many cases will far exceed the effort that many naturally slim people need to give when it comes to food over their lifetime.

There is an assumption that if you are slim you eat well...when many of us personally know people who have a healthy BMI but eat a terrible diet.

My research has shown that many overweight women have struggled with body image, weight gain, low self-esteem for a long long time, often starting the dieting process as teenagers, yoyo dieting, gaining weight through child-rearing, and then struggling to prioritise their own health.

Remember folks, 31 years is a long bloody time to be focused on one goal...and never managing to achieve it.

I spent at least 20 years actively trying to not be fat via dieting, but these days I absolutely do not diet because I know traditional dieting does not work for me. Nor does it work for hundreds of the women I work with.

So just to clarify my position on this, when I say I don't do dieting what I mean is:

- I don't restrict whole food groups, such as carbs or meat
- I don't go to weekly weigh-ins
- I don't weight myself weekly
- I don't follow a plan
- I am not either on or off my plan
- I am not good or bad according to what I have eaten
- I'm not part of a club or group
- I don't refer back to a book for guidance
- I don't buy special products
- I don't drink shakes or take pills

- I don't count calories
- I don't have a weight loss goal
- I don't hate myself as I currently am
- I don't believe life will be perfect when I am slimmer

This is not to say that I don't prioritise my health and general wellbeing. Food is a big part of that. Eating well is absolutely linked to the concept of living bigger: it enables me to fuel my body properly for running, it gives me energy for public speaking, it helps my hair and skin shine, it helps keep illness at bay. But what I don't ever do is use food primarily as a way of making me physically smaller at whatever cost.

There are some people who dislike and disagree with this approach, believing that to lose weight you simply have to "eat less and move more". There are also people who believe that concepts such as "Intuitive Eating", "Mindful Eating" or "Anti Dieting" are basically an excuse to just eat what the fuck we want, no matter the impact. leaving us to revel in our "I'm a body positive advocate" status.

This stuff is a minefield.

I don't "diet", but what I do pretty consistently is:

- Believe that food is primarily a fuel source for my body
- Think about the foods which make me feel good both physically and emotionally
- I do plan in my head what I might eat each week and sometimes each day
- I do look at labels, although I try to focus on foods which don't come in a packet
- I do look up recipes
- I do read about nutrition (but cautiously)
- I do batch cook
- I do keep an eye on how much water I am drinking
- I do keep tabs on my emotions and stress levels
- I do make sure I am eating enough to fuel my training and my lifetime
- I do focus on foods which are closest to their natural state
- I sometimes have foods that are not
- I do consult experts on nutrition
- I limit my alcohol intake, but also do not describe myself as a non-drinker
- I limit meat and dairy, but I am not a vegan

It has taken me a long long time to find a way of eating that appears to be working for me.

And when I say working I am not talking about weight loss, I am talking about feeling good within myself.

Not feeling hungry either physically or emotionally.
Not binging.
Not being on or off of my regime.
Not feeling like I can't have a life as well as look after myself.
Not feeling like I can't eat out.
Not feeing like life can resume once I get to goal weight….because remember, I don't have a goal weight…because I am NOT ON A DIET.

But remember the word DIET simply means "what we eat" and that may change throughout our lives according to all kinds of different factors. Our family, job, economic, and lifestyle circumstances, all play a part in the food choices we make. Later in the book when we talk about the three pillars of wellbeing, you will be encouraged to think about your food choices, because pretending that what we put in our mouth doesn't have an impact on our health, wealth or happiness is just foolish.

Check & Challenge 18: What is your dieting status?

Where are you at with the whole dieting idea? Are you still on and off your healthy eating and exercise habits? Are you still curious about the latest fads? Do you still attend a slimming club? Or follow a system? Are you ready to try a different way?

Don't worry, this is not the bit where I tell you what to eat or share with you my system.

I don't dish out nutritional advice to my coaching clients because I am not a nutritionist, but there are certain mindset concepts, therapeutic exercises, thought processes I have had to go through to get to this point of self-acceptance and empowerment - and there is value in sharing this with the women I work with.

I am also interested in the links between dieting and its impact on confidence, happiness and long-term health. For instance, if women stopped "dieting" and instead focused on learning to love their bodies as they are, then perhaps they might get on with the job of living an exciting, adventurous, purpose-filled life and through that process become stronger (physically and emotionally), fitter and healthier.

In the Spring of 2018, while researching for my TEDx talk I launched a new coaching programme to explore some of these concepts.

For years, women had been expressing to me their desires to lose weight in my running groups, asking for help with nutrition, setting and keeping to health goals, feeling better in themselves, and I didn't have the confidence to lead the programme because I didn't see myself as an expert.

But something shifted in the lead up to my TEDx, and I found myself saying:

"If I don't pull this programme together, who will?"

I recruited 100 women to work with me for 100 days to ditch the diet and to start focusing on health and happiness using 100 simple concepts that can be implemented daily and which contribute to a life filled with love and acceptance, self-care and understanding of our bodies. Most importantly, it aimed to give women a sense of hope that they can make peace with their bodies.

The programme explored five simple concepts, and gave women a safe online-community to share thoughts, update on progress and support one another. This combined to create some fantastic results for women: give examples here.

These results confirmed my belief that we should stop focusing on our bodies and give our mindset some attention instead.

I've used this pilot to create a seven-week programme called Stop Dieting, Start Living, which supports women to change their lives and how they feel about their bodies. *(Check out the link to this programme at the back of the book, its £97...just think of how much you have spent on dieting clubs over the years)*

Because we shouldn't be at war with our bodies.

We really shouldn't.

Is it acceptable to EVER want to be smaller?

Here is the tricky part.

Many people who follow body positive movements such as Health at Every Size, Fat Positivity, or FAT activism believe that any pursuit of smallness is out of line.

I believe this in itself is misleading and damaging.

For instance, I believe all humans at whatever weight they happen to be deserve respect and a life free of discrimination.

We should all have access to healthcare and support, regardless of our size.

However, it is also true that in some cases being fat is unhealthy and can contribute to increased risk of illnesses, such as diabetes, heart disease and high blood pressure.

You can't tell just by looking at someone if they are healthy or not, based on their size.

Dr Linda Bacon in her amazing book, "Health at Every Size: the surprising truth about your weight" says there is a widely held belief that:

"Drugs, surgery, a worthy person should do anything to win the weight loss game" but "understanding the reality behind these weight loss myths can be your journey towards salvation."

If you want to really look at the evidence base for not fat shaming someone, or believing that someone's weight is the most important factor to their health, spend some time reading Linda's work.

She quite provocatively says:

"This demonisation of fat flies in the face of not just psychology (calling people names never made anyone thin), but economics and medical science too. Persuasive, peer-reviewed evidence abounds that – hold onto your stethoscope – fat is blown out of proportion as a health risk and may actually confer some protection against early death."

I also believe something we don't always want to talk about is the fact that fatness can sometimes be a cry for help: overeating and not taking care of yourself can be seen as self-harm, a way of someone protecting themselves from something, or dealing with past trauma.

I don't know you and your story around weight gain.

I don't know your health stats

And I don't know the state of your mental health.

It is not my job to tell you whether your weight impacts on your health, what I do know is that for far too long I believed that being a size 18 was the worst thing in the world…nah, starving myself, not feeling accepted for the way I was, by the people that were supposed to love me and of course hating myself in an attempt to get to a size 12, that was far worse.

I spent far too long in that place.

This is not about weight loss at any cost through the hating of our current selves, or the following of regimes and programmes that do not support our wider health and happiness goals.

Yes, you may get smaller through the pursuit of healthy habits, and a change of lifestyle but what is most important is that we do not actively seeking smallness over and above everything else.

Can we love our self and still want to change?

We have a real problem in this world where millions of women spend the majority of their lives worrying about what dress size they are wearing and how they look to other people, irrespective of other success markers, such as health, wellbeing and happiness

The amount of times I said no to things in the past because I was on a diet, or I have put things off so I could wait for a time when I was smaller and therefore enjoy it properly. It can't be healthy to live life like that, waiting for life to happen when you reach goal weight - because of course living a happy and fulfilling life can only happen then.

Over the past 20 years I have been everything from a size 16 to a size 22. The majority of this time I have been a size 18 - a weight which feels comfortable, like it is potentially my set point weight.

I prefer for my weight to be stable. I can't stand the yo-yoing.

But as I get older my body is changing and I do notice aches and pains that perhaps could be alleviated by releasing some weight. Notice I didn't say losing? Losing implies loss and that it is inevitable that we will re-find it, something that makes us want to hold on to it even more somehow.

I would hate for women to get behind my movement, watch my TEDx, read this book and say to themselves:

"Julie's FAT she's awesome, therefore I can be FAT and awesome",

but then not pay attention to their overall health and happiness advice and find themselves wondering what happened a couple of years later. When we talk about self-awareness in the next chapter you will see how important it is to not be in denial about how your weight impacts on your health and happiness.

None of us really know what the impact of our weight will be on our future.

Me included.

So we must have the ability to decide for ourselves what we accept for our self...we get to decide what is healthy for us, and explore ways of reaching those health goals without traditional diets.

This is not the same as being in denial when your weight is clearly affecting your health, its more about telling people who have no idea what your other indicators of health look like that being overweight is bad for your health and must be addressed at any cost.

Remember the BIG traditional diet companies, and more recently all the internet-driven multi-level marketing companies that sell teas, shakes and bars... surely, if they were successful in helping people lose weight and keep it off, they wouldn't be in business?

It can sometimes seem as if they have a vested interest in keeping you fat, or at least you being in a cycle of being on and off their programmes, so they have a conveyor belt of customers.

It is often stated that 95% of dieters regain their weight in the first year after losing it, implying that it is near on impossible to ever lose weight and keep it off. I don't know if this is true or not. There is often conflicting evidence out there, some of which will have been funded by the very businesses whose profit-margins depend on people wanting to lose weight. It can be hard to know who to trust.

But what I do know is there are mixed messages everywhere we look when it comes to the effectiveness of dieting and different ways of eating. What works for one person doesn't work for everyone.

Even the original 95% failure rate isn't particularly robust. Dr. Kelly D. Brownell, the director of the Yale Center for Eating and Weight Disorders, said the number was first suggested in a 1959 clinical study of only 100 people and that the finding was repeated so often that it came to be regarded as fact.

I mean, it's a useful stat to throw in the face of anyone who suggests you join Slimming World for the 10th time, isn't it.

Since then, nearly all studies of weight-loss have followed patients in formal hospital or university programs, because they are the easiest to identify and keep track of. But people who turn to such programs may also be the most difficult cases, and may therefore have especially poor success rates.

Two researchers studying long-term dieters for a project called the National Weight Control Registry in the US have found it surprisingly easy to collect success stories. About half the people who maintained a substantial weight loss for more than a year had done it on their own, they found. This suggests that many people have found ways to lose weight and keep it off, but have never been counted in formal studies.

Whether the research exists or does not, our own experiences and those around us clearly show that what we have been doing hasn't worked. The slimming clubs, the diet books, the restriction, the self-loathing, the putting life on hold, the starting again on Monday, the having a treat night, the starving and then binging.

It is exhausting. Do we want to be slim? Or do we just want to be happy and healthy? Could we focus on that instead?

Could we stop setting measures of success which are to do with scales, tape measures and clothing sizes and instead make up our own markers of health and happiness that are more to do with confidence levels, ability to function affectively, and to lead a lifestyle fitting to our hopes and desires?

What do you think? Look I get it. Women often turn to dieting when they get to a place in their life where they are truly unhappy. Going on a diet seems like something tangible they can do to regain some kind of control. But there are other ways, I promise you.

Many of us reach a point in life where we come to a cross roads, where we think "right, that's it, I can't take any more", where we feel in the pit of our bellies that we are ready for change. I know, I've been there.

Sometimes it is triggered by a significant life moment, a birth or a death, sometimes it's from a health scare, and sometimes it's nothing major - just an underlying feeling that you are not really living.

Instead of turning to dieting, we need to turn towards self-love and using the resources we normally use on dieting on other self-development practices. There are enough to chose from. I don't think people really want perfect, aesthetically pleasing bodies, certainly after a certain age, I just think women want to feel ok in the skin that they are in, free of judgment and ridicule.

Often the frustration and anger we feel about our bodies is misguided because of the yo-yoing and the sense of this not being something we are able to control.

We need to be a little kinder to ourselves.

We need to see what we have put our bodies through over the years, and how they have supported us regardless, instead of believing that they have let us down. Are you ready to do some of this important non-diet related self-improvement work?

Are you ready to finally make peace with yourself

Self-Awareness

Are you ready to accept who you truly are yet?

Do you know who you are?

Who you really are?

Do you like who you are?

Are you friends with you?

Like seriously, how much time do you even spend with you?

I am not just talking about how much time you spend on your own, because that is something completely different. I am talking about how comfortable you are with being really present with your self.

The person who you truly are.

When is the last time you sat yourself down and listened to what you have to say? Come on ladies, we all know what it feels like to be in a relationship or friendship that is one sided, where we don't feel valued, don't feel listened to.

Surely it is time to address the fact that we are kind of being that person to ourselves.
As women when we talk about self-love and self-acceptance, it is often in the context of how we feel. I think we've got this all wrong. You don't have to feel like you are in love with yourself, you just have to act like you do.

There is a difference.

How many times have you screamed at a partner: "I don't need you to tell me that you
love me, I need you to show me" Or is that just me?

The most powerful thing I ever learned (and I can't even remember where I learned it) was that love is a verb.

It is a doing word.

Remember that from school? Doing words.

Love is an act of will, both an intention and an action. Will also implies choice. We do not have to love. We choose to love. And we can choose to love our self.

Have you ever been in a relationship which is on its dying legs, one where there is perhaps a sense of duty to let it go on even though you know it has come to its natural end? It could even be a friendship or a relationship you have with a family member. There comes a point where you have to remind yourself that you have a choice: you don't have to love someone who is mean to you or who doesn't love you back.

You can walk away. Hide away. Or bit by bit you can rebuild, either with them in your life or with someone completely new. You can choose to love someone in a new way. You can choose to love yourself differently.

However, before we can love ourselves properly, we have to understand ourselves, and we can't understand ourselves if we are not willing to be self aware, and spend some quality time together. Much like any relationship.

Check & Challenge 19 – How much do you love yourself?

In your journal, write a list of the things that you do daily, weekly, monthly that illustrate the love you have for yourself. Also write down how it feels to even consider loving yourself, and if that is too strong perhaps use the phrase liking yourself instead.

We will get to some practical ways for to love yourself more radically later, (and no it isn't anything naughty) but for now let's just stick with the awareness piece for a while.

I find through my work that some women are more self-aware than others.

Some can get to who they are, the things which drive them, their backstory, their values and beliefs quite quickly and with ease, while others haven't done any of this work for such a long time, or maybe even at all that it feels alien.

Many resist getting to know themselves at all.

Some have long since decided they are not even likeable, let alone loveable, so they avoid spending time in their own head.

However, the biggest transformations I see in women are where they are willing to try something new, or to revisit a tool or technique they had dismissed in the past. Where they are willing to be uncomfortable for a while, willing to spend some time on healing themselves, becoming a slightly different person, willing to grow.

Are you a spiritual being?

Now this is where I get a bit "woo woo" on you. If you are not sure what the term "woo woo" even is, oh boy, are we going to have some fun in this chapter.

I never really considered myself a spiritual being until recently. I don't know if this is because I was raised a Catholic amongst quite a bunch of negative "You get what you given" and "You live and then you die" kinda people.

But I always had a fascination with people and what motivated them. What makes them tick?

As a child I had various attempts at keeping a diary, I managed to write every day for a year when I was 16. Reading that back is a little depressing because I was hugely unaware of who I was back then. Perhaps we all were at that age...my writing was all about the boys I fancied that never looked at me, and how unfair the world was.

But over time I have become more open to different spiritual concepts and ideas of which I do not completely understand in their entirety. I am 100% open to learning and giving more of these a go in the pursuit of improved health, wealth and happiness.

The internet has opened up this world to us significantly over the past few decades. Films such as "The Secret" and the success of big personal development figures such as Tony Robbins, Louise Hay, Oprah Winfrey and Lisa Nichols have opened our eyes up to the world of changing your mindset and working on yourself.

Back in 2014, when my life was literally crumbling around me, reading books and articles, and listening to audiobooks by these folks filled my head with ideas that gave me hope and which took me away from the hopelessness of my life at that time.

I was unemployed and looking after a small baby with nothing to occupy my time or my thinking capacity, so I visited the local library daily and read as much as I could. These books were a lifeline, helping me to believe that things could change.

The U.S. self-improvement market was worth $9.9 billion in 2016, and in the UK, the self-help book industry alone is estimated to be worth at least £6 million.

Now clearly this is big business, but also what an opportunity to shift our thinking?

There is a whole army of people ready to knock personal development and mock it, saying that it has no value, that it's snake oil, and that the people leading this area are just money-hungry, ego-maniacs.

But before we dismiss it as mumbo jumble and pseudo-science, I want to encourage you to be open to the idea that, if nothing else, these practices can help people feel better about themselves, feel more connected with themselves and with others, much like mainstream religion or belonging to some other kind of organized thinking does.

These self-development practices are what have supported me over the past few years to really grow as a leader, as a coach, but also as a mother, a daughter, a sister, a friend.

They really are the gift that keeps on giving.

For me though, it was when I finally got my head around the "Law of attraction" concept that I started to see the biggest impact.

What is the Law of Attraction?

Simply put the Law of Attraction is the ability to attract into our lives whatever we are focusing on, both positive and negative.

It is simply about energy.

Albert Einstein famously said:

"Everything is energy, and that's all there is to it. Match the frequency of the reality you want and you cannot help but get that reality. It can be no other way. This is not philosophy, this is physics."

Think it and it will happen is a very simplistic way of explaining the Law of Attraction, but those who believe in it, reckon it is that straight forward.

I know this can be a lot to get your head around.

Especially the idea that if there are bad things happening in your life that you have asked for it, or at least attracted it somehow. It is still something I struggle with - although growing up I guess "Sods Law" was kind of what this was. We believed that something bad would happen and it did. We would take great pleasure in saying "I told you so" when it did.

Over the last few years I have become a convert, as increasingly I have been able to witness the Law of Attraction for myself just by becoming more self-aware. If I focus on doom and gloom, I remain in that dark space where I attract even shittier things into my life, whereas when I focus on the good in my life, more seems to arrive.

The Law of Attraction is about sitting back and thinking without judgement or restraint of all the things you want to appear into your life so they land on your lap. It is also about holding things clearly in your minds eye, feeling all of the feelings that are associated with the thing, and then – importantly - taking inspired action that helps draw them to you.

Check & Challenge 20 – Are you a believer in the Law of Attraction?

Can you think of things that you have attracted into your life in this way? Do you believe that your vibe and what you focus on attracts energy both good and bad? Is the law of attraction something you are willing to explore in more detail?

I have always been super interested in coincidences and also the idea of karma.

I found it reasonably easy as a teenager and young adult to believe that for every action there is a reaction, and that there are powers beyond those that we can see, know and understand that are at play in our day-to-day life.

When I was in my early 20s, I started spotting coincidences and things that seemed to happen for a reason. For example, while working in a theatre bar, I met a club promoter who gave my sister and me two free tickets for a trendy club in Shoreditch, London.

When I arrived and asked for this guy at the door, I have never seen someone so excited to see someone else in a nightclub. He greeted me and my sister, bought us a drink and then introduced us to tallest, most scariest-looking bouncer you have ever met - I can remember thinking "Shit I'm in trouble."

Anyway, long story short, it turned out that this bouncer and the club promoter had both been in the theatre at the same time as my shift a few weeks back. The bouncer had spotted me, although I hadn't seen him. Unbeknown to him, his club promoter friend had noticed some kind of weird attraction thing going on and decided to arrange for us to meet. His observation was correct - I ended up dating this bouncer for around the next two years on and off, and in many ways he became a bit of a spiritual teacher. He was the first guy who I could ever really talk to about life, about my aspirations, about the world.

The bouncer also introduced me to a book called The Celestine Prophecy, which opened my eyes up to all kind of ideas. I didn't see the world in the same way after reading that book, I didn't see people or the way they interacted the same.

I started reading more.

I began to question the world I lived in and my place in it.

I am not going to pretend this was a straight-sailing journey towards spiritual enlightenment, because it absolutely was not. But over the last 20 years I have become increasingly aware of, and interested in, alternative therapies and spiritual practices, which previously I would have been super skeptical of.

Over the last five years, these practices have absolutely changed my life. Partly because I have allowed them to but also because my circle of friends and colleagues are either spiritual coaches, energy workers or people simply on a similar journey to me, a journey towards being more satisfied in life, which means they understand me and I don't feel like such a freak talking about this stuff with them.

In this chapter, I want to share with you five tools and techniques I use regularly to stay connected with myself, but also to continually improve my health, wealth and happiness. I don't do these things religiously, and I could always give them more time and attention, but they are always there to support me especially when life gets tough or I feel overwhelmed.

Please note, I am not suggesting you *have* to take up all or any of these "options". You may feel they are not for you or you may find alternative practices, therapies or activities that are more suitable to your journey. But I do want you to start thinking about the fact you have them - options that is.

Remember ladies...it is OK not to be OK, but it's not OK to wallow in self-pity and not make some kind of effort to work through whatever it is you have going on. Working out the options you have available to you to feel better will change your life.

Option 1 - Mirror Work

This is the most power piece of work you can do when it comes to self-awareness and self-love, and is so incredibly simple to do.

Yet I have found so many women are resistant to it.
Mirror Work was designed by the late Louise Hay who says of this work:
"For most of us, sitting in front of a mirror and facing ourselves is difficult at first, so we call this process mirror WORK. *But as you continue, you become less self-critical, and the work turns into mirror play. Very soon your mirror becomes your companion, a dear friend instead of an enemy."*

Imagine that being able to look into the thing that for so many years we have tried to avoid, or used as a tool to beat our selves up.

The first step is allowing yourself to have mirrors in your home. Many of us actively avoid them and find we don't even own a full-length mirror anymore, or have conveniently hid them or covered them with clutter.

It doesn't have to be a full-length mirror; you may find a small handheld one slightly more intimate. It starts with simply looking at yourself.

Trying to look at yourself but without judgment, not looking for the flaws.Looking at things that you like and appreciate.

Or simply looking with a view to accept and acknowledge what we see.

Through this work you are going to be reminded of the most important relationship you will ever have: the one you have with yourself.

The way I practice mirror work is in two parts and can be done in really small amounts of time, or in a more extended way once you want to go deeper.

Be sure you are sitting comfortably.
Look into the mirror. Look into your eyes. Inhale deeply.
That is part one - simply taking the time to look.

Part two is to say something to your reflection, my favorite phrase being: "You are enough".
Some people suggest you say something such as "I love you" but that can be quite overwhelming at first.

One of Louise's favourite affirmations is "Life Loves You", which is also a good reminder.

After you have spoken your words, exhale. It's good to keep breathing throughout.

Repeat the phrases a number of times and notice your response each time. Pay attention to sensations of the body, feelings in your heart, and mental commentary.

You can write these in your journal.

Feelings may include sadness and grief; hope and happiness. Thoughts may include commentary such as I can't do this, and this is stupid. But stick with it and try not to judge your responses.

I do this exercise with women in my programmes, and they are always surprised at how powerful it can be.

Lorna said:

Dropped daughter off at dance class today, studio has floor to ceiling mirrors on 3 of the walls. Usually I make sure not to look at myself AT ALL! But today I made sure I looked at myself, did I look like a super model? No. But actually I look alright, just like a regular Mum doing regular Mum things, nothing to see here. Really made me feel good to:
a) actually look in the mirror
b) not be horrified/upset etc at what I saw

Check & Challenge 21 – What do you see when you look in the mirror?

How often do you look in the mirror? What do you see? What affirmations can you create to change the soundtrack that normally plays when you look at the mirror? How can you make mirror work fun and playful?

Option 2 - Yoga
I have a real love/hate relationship with yoga, or indeed any kind of slow contemplative movement, but it is something I have tried time and time again over the years with varying success.

When I went to a class at my local gym when I was in my 20s, I remember being annoyed by the instructor. I was a bit like: "Oh just shut up and get on with it."

I tried videos at home, I had a few books and from time to time I would do little bits but I never really got it. I knew that if I could stick with it the benefits for my general wellbeing and for my running would be fab. However, I was having difficulty finding the time and the inclination to make it part of my life. Plus, people like me didn't do yoga...or so I thought.

Then the concept of plus-size yoga became more prominent on social media a few years back and I started to see bodies similar to mine doing it. I also came across the incredibly inspiring, Jessamyn Stanley.

Jessamyn is a yoga instructor, body positive advocate and writer based in North Carolina. She used a style of yoga called Vinyasa as a way to move past mental and emotional barriers, using a body positive approach that celebrates students' bodies and encourages them to ask "How do I feel" rather than "How do I look" when practicing yoga.

Back in 2016, a string of coincidences led me to meeting Jessamyn at a Q&A session she was doing while she was in the UK. It was a small intimate gathering held at the Siobhan Davies Dance Studios in Elephant and Castle.
I admit that at first I felt like a bit of a fraud really, being the novice at yoga that I am.

So in the week leading up to meeting Jessamyn, I did more practice than I had in the last 10 years – the result being that I could actually see improvements in simple (yet challenging) poses such as my Downward Dog.

On the day of the event, Jessamyn was just awesome. This is not just because I love her accent. I loved how honest she was, the way she cursed but would also be articulate and thought-provoking. Her comments were considered enough to know she had thought them through and yet there was no huge display of ego, which was refreshing.

One thing she said was: "When you stop yourself on a yoga mat, you know you are stopping yourself in other areas in life".

This just really struck a chord.

How true is that? How often have you thought:

"Oh this is hard, let me stop and do something else."
"I can't do what she can do so there's no point."
"Let me just watch TV instead."

It can be easy to spot the self-sabotage and upper limit beliefs that we sometimes have when we are trying to change or create new habits.

Take yoga as an example.

Often on the yoga mat I am like "urghhh, that's starting to hurt now", or "OK I'm bored that's enough" even though I know that I will only feel the benefit of it if I stick with it for longer periods of time.

When looking at people doing yoga poses, it can be easy to think "I can never do that" and so never even attempt them. But how do you know if you haven't tried? What else in life might you be able to do but those limiting beliefs are stopping you before you have even given it a go.

As the evening progressed, there were lots of questions about visibility and Jessamyn said:

"I had no idea I was supposed to be doing this, but now I know there's nothing else I should be doing."
A statement that I 100% also believe about my own work.
She then said:
"It didn't need to be me but it had to be someone."

Because there was nobody else doing the work she was doing.
I then got the opportunity to ask my question. However, before I had finished introducing myself and admitting I wasn't really a Yogi but a plus-size runner, Jessamyn interrupted me and was like "OMG it's YOU!!!!!!"

I didn't for a minute think she would know who I was and apparently she did. It was a really exciting, fun and slightly uncomfortable moment.

She told me I was one of the people who influenced her decision to be more visible online.

The power of the internet, hey?

Being in the public eye on social media can be really challenging. You are often accused of being a show off, or publicity hungry, or that your ego is out of control. You have daily battles with yourself, questioning "WHO CARES" and why am I posting all this stuff about what I think, what I do and "Why is it even important". But it is.

Jessamyn then said something which really made me want to cry a bit. She said:

"When I was 12, I just wanted someone to tell me it's OK to be exactly how you are."

So many of us can connect with that feeling.

The way sports and physical activities are marketed and presented to us can be a problem. It's often about this perceived lifestyle, or a pursuit of the perfect body. Or it is often about specific goals, such as running a marathon or doing a headstand.

All of this means we miss the crucial point: it's about the journey. It's about the daily practice, it's about the connection you make between your body and your soul regardless of any of that other crap that sports brands want to force upon us.

Ultimately it's about looking in rather than looking out, and being comfortable with who you are as a person, making peace with yourself.

That sounds like Living a Bigger life to me, what do you think?

Check & Challenge 22 – What has been your experience of yoga?

Is it something you are willing to commit to moving forward? Is it a practice which you could see working in your life to support your health, wealth and happiness goals? How could you integrate this into your current life? Is there another 'sport' that you could introduce into your life that will help you look inwards rather than out?

Option 3 - Tapping or Emotional Freedom Technique

Now I have to confess, this is a practice where I really do not understand how it works. It is a practice that I struggle with doing consistently. But what I do know, is that when I use it, it 100% works for me, which is why I call upon it quite frequently during moments of high stress and is a practice I have passed onto my daughter, Rose.

Emotional Freedom Technique (EFT), or Tapping as it is often known, is a self-help technique that involves tapping near the end points of "energy meridians" located around the body in order to reduce tension and promote a deeper mind-body connection.

The way I have always used it is for releasing fears or insecurities, literally calling out the stuff I am most worrying about and accepting that even if that stuff happens I will still be OK. It has really helped me calm down before big talks and when I have faced big "now what" blocks in my business.

Apparently it's EFT's ability to access the amygdala, an almond-shaped part of your brain that initiates your body's negative reaction to fear, a process we often refer to as the "fight or flight" response, that makes it so powerful.

EFT accesses the body's various meridian points, points in the body where energy flows, much like how acupuncture works...but this doesn't involve needles and is completely painless.

You don't have to be an EFT practitioner, have a coach, or understand how it works for it to work, and you can simply follow other people's scripts or make up your own. I started off watching a guy called Brad Yates on his YouTube Channel, "Tap with Brad". It felt weird at first because it was new, but it also felt extra weird for me because:

A.   He is a bloke
B.   He is American

I wanted to find a woman I could relate to who did what Brad did.

And this led me to find a wonderful EFT and energy worker called Marie Houlden, a woman from the UK who I had a much better connection with and who has since become a friend and colleague, supporting some of my online programmes with tapping sessions.

She has some wonderful scripts about loving yourself, overcoming self-limiting beliefs and bringing in more abundance.

I am part of one of Marie's programmes that give you access to all of her recordings, and often when I am feeling stuck I start my day tapping along to one of her scripts.

When I am out and about, often before speaking gigs or important meetings I take myself off somewhere private and follow a very simple script of:

Even though, *insert fear here* I love and accept myself.

This often looks like:

"Even though this is a really important speaking gig, and I am completely under-rehearsed and am going to look like an absolute dick on the stage when I fuck it up, I love and accept myself".

———

I say this over and over again, until I no longer fear it actually happening.

I tap on the outside of my hand and on my forehead mainly, but there are more meridian points that can be used, such as under your nose, and under your armpit.

If I can't say the mantras out loud, I simply say them in my head and tap discreetly on the outside of my hand.

With my daughter Rose, I often use tapping at bed time or when she is being difficult. It helps her to connect to her feelings and also helps me to be calmer and more present with her, so it really is a win-win.

A typical script with Rose would be something like:

"Even though I don't want to go to bed, I love and accept myself."
"Even though I am scared of monsters, I love and accept myself."
"Even though the girls at school were being mean to me, I love and accept myself."

I love how empowered Rose feels when doing EFT and how she loves to share this with her cousins (who often look at her like she is bonkers but they know she's my daughter and that Auntie Julie is a bit weird).

The thing with EFT, much like all of these techniques, is that it feels weird at first, and you may have resistance or simply forget to do them. However, it is a practice, you don't have to be perfect in your use of them, and the more you do them the more powerful they become and the more they can impact positively impact on your life.

Check & Challenge 23 – Are you up for some EFT?

Use one of the scripts off YouTube, either from Brad or Marie or anyone else you find that you like, and see how you feel. Choose a script that resonates with how you are feeling, or what you are most stuck with and see how you get on. Think about some simple scripts you could come up with to help you over come fear or resistance.

Option 4 - Hypnosis

Hypnosis has long been associated as being a potential solution for weight loss, thanks to Paul McKenna's popular book "I can make you thin" and more recently Marissa Peer's book of a similar title.

I have heard lots of stories about women losing weight through this method. For me, I am less interested in hypnosis for weight loss but more in terms of it helping you to understand your stories and the way you think about things.

I first went to see a hypnotherapist around 15 years ago for weight loss. It was a rather rushed experience with a hypnotist I only ever saw once. I didn't quite like his attitude as he looked at me as someone who was broken and needed fixing, and that he was my solution.

I don't think that is the case for anyone.

I was interested in how it all worked though, as it did work. Over the 90-minute session he asked me for three key pieces of information, no backstory, no time to understand me fully, just three simple pieces of information.

1. Someone who I hold resentment to...I didn't even need to tell him who
2. A food which I would like to give up
3. The food which is the most problematic to my health

The first thing that he worked on for about 90 seconds or so was the resentment I held about my dad. It was probably the first time I admitted to someone that I felt like this; I didn't talk about my dad leaving us for a long time. It was still very raw even 10 years on.

Anyway, with one simple exercise he took my resentment level from a nine out of 10 to a six. I can't really remember exactly what he did but it involved following a pen with my eyes.
It instantly changed how I felt about my dad. Not just how I thought about him but how I felt. Something shifted in my heart.

He then focused on the specific foods I was addicted to, but what he didn't take the time to really understand was that I was addicted to all foods. My disordered eating was at its worst back then; I hadn't even started to address my shit yet.

I was just looking for a solution to my unhappiness, and I thought weight loss would be it.

First, we looked at a recent habit I had picked up. Buying a packet of Malteasers every night at the train station on the way home from work, and sometimes a pack at 3pm when the tea trolley came round at work.

He got me to picture these surrounded with my least favorable substance and, of course, I chose shit. Yes, those round chocolate covered biscuit balls covered in excrement. It doesn't take much to summon up an image, or maybe even an imagined taste, texture or smell to put you off that confectionary for ever.

Even sitting here typing this I can feel saliva forming in my mouth as though I was about to vomit. That association has never left me; I have not eaten them since.

The final thing he worked on was the one where we spent the most amount of time, where I actually went under so to speak. He hypnotized me to not be physically able to eat crisps - a food that I had no control over.

I went under so I can't tell you what he did but let me tell you it was super powerful.
For the next six months, I couldn't be within a three-metre proximity to a potato-based snack. I had to avoid the aisle in the supermarket and leave the room if someone was eating them. Even if I thought about them a weird sensation happened in my stomach and throat to the point where I thought I might be sick.

Despite this session being over 15 years ago I can still evoke that response.

However, about three years after being hypnotized, I was at a friend's house for lunch and she brought out some corn chips to eat with some dip, and I ate them without thinking.

Over time I have been able to eat crisps again, and there have been times where I have binged on them again, but with a little bit of focus I can reconnect with those initial feelings and convince myself not to eat them - even mid packet.

This experience of hypnotherapy was only one aspect of what I have learned about it, and possibly not the most useful in my view.

Since then I have worked more extensively with two separate female hypnotherapists who use a process called Rapid Transformation Therapy. This is the same method that Marisa Peer uses very successfully and which incorporates the most effective components of Hypnotherapy, NLP, CBT and Psychotherapy.

These two specific coaches have supported my online programmes and retreats, and are both ladies who I have used to support my ongoing journey towards improved health and happiness rather than specifically losing weight.

This more in-depth work has enabled me to recall stories from my childhood that were long since forgotten, and helped me to re-programme the way I think and feel about some of my experiences.

I think the fact these therapists were women who had both experienced weight gain, was helpful in them understanding me better.

Is hypnotherapy the solution for weight loss?

Some people achieve weight loss using hypnotherapy. However, I believe that it is best used as a tool to help you better understand your issues as part of a wider self-acceptance journey.

You can also self-hypnotize, so this isn't necessarily about hiring an expensive coach.

Out of all the things I have tried to help me feel better about myself, hypnotherapy has without a doubt been the most powerful, but I think this is in part because I also developed wonderful friendships over a longer period of time with these women - and I realised in some ways I was craving that deeper connection with women I could share my story with.

One of the most significant breakthroughs happened in a session I had a few months ago with a wonderful therapist called Glyniss Trinder, who under hypnosis gently took me back to a number of incidents from my childhood, some of which I have shared throughout this book.

The one that triggered the biggest breakthrough was a memory of being around the age of 10 and being at home waiting for my dad to come home with food or money to buy food so we could eat. We were all hungry, and in the end it got so late that we had to go to bed without dinner.

I can remember asking my mum about this incident during an argument a few years later and she denied it even happened. I can understand why. The point is it doesn't even really matter any more, because it wasn't about the food, it was about the feeling of lack, and the feeling of being uncared for.

When I came round from hypnosis I said to Glynnis that this story summed up how I had felt my whole life. It was always feast or famine in our house, and that has very much been the case in other areas of my life over the years, in love, with friendships and financially as I have been developing my business - moments of real struggle followed by moments of real abundance, and then the cycle starts again.

Can you see how these things can be linked and how self-development and spiritual practices can help you unlock understanding?

I will discuss this connection with food and finance more in a further chapter.

Check & Challenge 24 – Are you ready to be hypnotized?

Have you ever been under hypnosis? Do you believe it could unlock some further understanding and awareness for you, and perhaps reprogram the way you think? Perhaps start with one of the books that come with FREE hypnosis recordings and see how you get on.

Option 5 - Cards

If you are a little bit overwhelmed or frightened by the practices I have suggested so far, or you haven't got the time or money to commit to working with a coach, or don't really believe they can work, here is something else for you to consider.

This one is a very simple technique that can help shift your energy in an instant, and where the investment starts at around £12.99.

I bought my first set of angel cards about three years ago.

I had seen lots of coaches online using them and thought it might be a fun activity to do.
With my first pack of chakra cards, I played around with a few layouts to answer specific questions I had about the direction my life was heading in.
Cards tend to come with a little instruction book, so you don't need any specific talents or skill to use them, although people who do readings will memorise the meanings and be able to make sense of card combinations, etc.

I have great fun with my sister Jennie under the influence of alcohol asking the angels if we are ever going to get married or become millionaires.

I now have six packs, from various creators, and the questions I ask are far more sophisticated these days.

My favourite sets are:

1. Rebecca Campbell's – Work Your Light Oracle Cards
2. Gabby Bernstein's – The Universe Has your Back Cards

These packs are based on books from the authors in question, and I would recommend reading them too if you are looking for somewhere to start on this spiritual path.

The way I use the cards include

- Pulling a card each day to set an intention

- Pulling a card when I have a decision to make
- Pulling a card when I feel anxious or resistance

I would say every 12 weeks or so I spend an evening at home doing some more detailed spreads to get answers based on current developments and plans.

What I don't do is rely on these readings as business advice. I have robust business strategies and processes to keep me on track in this area of my life. Instead, the cards help me get my mindset in check in a way business books don't.

I used to be super skeptical about fortune tellers and tarot cards. My mum once went to one who said one of her kids were going to have a bad cycle accident, which then meant we weren't allowed to have our bikes that summer, which was a bit annoying. She also said my mum would meet and marry a fireman but she never did.

However, recently I had a random 30-minute card reading at a Wellbeing Show and I was blown away by how accurate the reading was. All I gave this woman was my name, yet the things she told me were so detailed. For example:

1. That I had just that week had a big success in my business, hitting a big financial target. *I had just made £10,000 in 10 days launching a new programme.*
2. In two weeks time, you will be taking an important message to a global stage. *This was two weeks before my TEDx talk.*
3. Recently a family member who has been missing for a long time got back in touch, and he is living in a hot country. *My dad had just got in touch via email from the Middle East after being out of my life for more than 20 years.*
4. That my ex-partner and father of my daughter was a black man, who was on the stage. *He is indeed an actor from West Indian descent.*
5. That I was currently single and too busy for love, but that I would find someone later in the year that would also be an entrepreneur. *Well, I will keep an eye out for him, ha ha!*

There were other things too, and all completely spot on without me revealing anything about who I was.

I know this stuff isn't for everyone, but what I would say is if something like this gives you hope, or helps you better understand yourself, then why not?

In Chapter 8, I will talk more about how you can use these clues and prompts to help attract the things you want into your life, to speed up the process so to speak.

Check and Challenge 25 – Pull a Card

How do you feel about tarot, oracle, angel or any other kind of cards? If you have a set at home, dig them out and pull yourself a card for additional motivation, courage, direction or support.

Hopefully you will find some of these supporting practices, these options helpful in your onward journey.

Often we want a solution to the challenges we face in our lives immediately, but we don't really want to do the work.

Remember though, we are the way we are due to a lifetime of experiences and life lessons which have shaped us after years and years of thinking and feeling in certain ways.

To change, we have to change.

We have to be able to unpack, restore and heal so that we can move forward.

Bringing new rituals into your life, no matter how silly they may feel at the time could offer you an alternative way of living, if only to give you five minutes of peace and quiet.

How about asking some of your friends, colleagues, family members what things they do just for themselves, to relax, to reconnect with themselves? You might be surprised how many people are working on themselves in private.

Check & Challenge 26 – What other alternative therapies and coaching practices could you try?

Make a list in your journal of other ways you can connect with yourself. Do a bit of research on the following, all of which I have tried over the years. A quick search on Google will reveal what they are and how to do them if these are new to you:
- Reiki
- Morning Pages
- Meditation
- Tai Chi
- Crystals

- Homeopathy
- Acupuncture
- Massage

Anything that gives you time out, time to think, time to just be will help you connect with yourself. Exercise is a great one of these, especially a solo sport such as running or yoga...and especially when done as self-care not purely for weightloss reasons.

Time to start working on the most important relationship you will ever have.

I know it sounds clichéd that the relationship we have with our self is the most important one of all but it is.

Too often we stick our heads in the sand and don't even want to think about what that means.

I think as women we struggle with self-awareness because we are carers, nurturers, supporters, and spend far too much time considering the needs of others.

Ultimately, we have forgotten how to put our own needs first.

As if having your own wants and desires is selfish.

I see this all the time in my coaching groups.

We talk a lot about emotional labour, and the inequality of household and parenting duties in our homes. Quite often when women share in our groups that they are struggling to cope, it is often due to massive overwhelm of having so much on their plates.

Women post things such as:

"It's 10am and already I have got two kids out of bed, fed, dressed and off to school with all the right stuff, written a funding application that was due today, located various lost items for the husband, cooked tonight's dinner, cleaned the kitchen, unloaded and loaded the washing machine, briefed the builders and ordered an outfit for my friends wedding which is next weekend, and had a half hour call with social services about mum's care plan. Now for a day at work."

We can't nor should we be expected to do EVERYTHING. All that does is leave us exhausted, burnt out, undervalued and maybe even resentful.

Part of the Living Bigger philosophy is around curating a life that fills you with joy. Often that involves tackling some of the crap that isn't working right and finding ways to readdress the balance.

This sometimes means having some pretty difficult conversations with your loved ones, work colleagues and friends, and being able to clearly articulate your needs.

One of the ladies from my Living a Bigger Life online coaching programme experienced this recently with her husband:

"I found myself doing everything: cooking, cleaning, organizing both our lives and this was on top of my regular 12-hour working days. Meanwhile, my husband wasn't working and would instead be found either out on his bike, playing computer games or drinking wine. I started feeling really angry and resentful towards him. I tried asking him to help relieve my load but he didn't hear me. I found myself drinking more as a coping mechanism. Then one day, during a drunken argument, I lost it and threw a glass of wine at him. I'm never violent and I hated that I had resorted to that. Something had to change. We had a big long chat and I learned that he had deliberately been trying to stay out of my way because I was stressed and wasn't so pleasant to be around. He thought that this was to do with my work and hadn't clocked that it was because he wasn't pulling his weight. I am so glad we had that conversation (although I wish it hadn't been instigated by me losing the plot). He now does much more around the house, and if I ever start to feel overwhelmed, I raise it much sooner and he is much more understanding about what he needs to do to help."

Let's face it we live in a world of "comparisonitus" when it comes to women and the lives they live. We read in magazines what we should be juggling, and see images on the TV of well put together women doing all manor of exciting things.

How do they fit it all in?

They must just be better at life than us, right?

We think everyone out there has got it sussed, have found the answers to life and can easily perform at these high levels with effortless cool yet we can only see the staggering shortfall in ourselves and our lives.

Perhaps we are all just winging it? Doing the best that we can.

Or perhaps we are all different and have a different set of values, skills, talents and abilities, and different resources available to us. We want different things from our life so how can we be expected to all act like cookie cutter forms of the same thing?

It's like people who are able to keep a clean, tidy and clutter free home.

I will never understand how they do it.

Like NEVER.

It doesn't matter how many times I tidy up, get in help to declutter, hire a cleaner...I am naturally a messy person, and there are simply just too many other things far more important to me than having a shelf devoid of nick naks or shoes in the hallway.

Getting clear on your values is a wonderfully empowering process, because it gives you the
chance to let go of stuff that you don't actually care that much about anyway.

It helps you to stop the pretense, and not have to keep up with other people.

For years my mum, my ex and various other people tried to make me feel bad for not ironing my clothes.

If ironing is your thing, great. It is not something I care about.

I mainly buy clothes that don't need ironing, fold them in a way that minimizes creases and when I do need to iron of course I do, but you won't find me every Sunday night standing for hours breaking my back ironing like my Mum used to.

Growing up, one of my aunties always had a messy car. In fact she used to pay me £5 a time to clear it out. She would sit and drink cups of tea with my mum while I headed out to the car with a black bag, a duster and the hoover.

Some of my family used to turn their noses up and say she was lazy. I guess, I kind of agreed. On reflection, what did I know back then? I'd never tried to raise 3 kids, with a full-time job and have interests of my own.

We get to choose how we spend our time, what we focus on, what we find an acceptable way of living.

Check & Challenge 27 – What are your values

List five to 10 things that are super important to you? And then list them in order or importance. Remember, you do not need to be a martyr, plus nobody has to see this list except you, if you don't want.

So if calling your mother-in-law is not as important as catching up on Love Island (cough cough, I mean self care) hey I'm not judging.

If I had been able to have more clarity on the things I wanted in my life earlier, I may not have wasted so much time trying to be someone I clearly wasn't, and probably would have avoided so many domestic arguments with my daughter's dad. We clearly had different value and ideas about how to live our lives, it would have saved us a whole heap of grief and heartache.

In Chapter 9 we will look more into what motivates us, but for now I just want you to open up to the suggestion that some of these practices where implemented daily or even more sporadically can help you connect with yourself.

I want you to commit to ear-marking more time for you.

I want you to commit to building on your relationship with yourself, journaling, thinking, connecting up the dots.

For you to serious improve your health, wealth and happiness in order to live a bigger life, you have to start by truly reviewing what these concepts mean to you, and be able to really see without judgment where you are with each of them.

So let's see where we are shall we?

The 3 Pillars of Wellbeing

"I don't know what I want or even what I need,
but all I know is I have to feel better than I do right now.

Let me ask you a question.

What is it to feel well?

To feel alive?

To feel like you are not just surviving but actually thriving?

Stop and think about if for a while?

Is it about happiness? Is it about health? Is it about life panning out how you expected it to or having the resources available to fulfil your goals?

Is it all of these things?

Or are we too preoccupied with this whole idea of wellness?

What even does it mean?

The World Health Organization defines wellness as a state of complete physical, mental, and social wellbeing, and in a 2017 report revealed that the "wellness industry" is worth a whopping $3.7 trillion.

So BIG BUSINESS!!!!

No wonder so many people are ramming the wellness agenda down our throats.

I often wonder what my grandparents would have made of the work I do now.

Both lived well into their 70s, on a diet of fried food, 40 unfiltered fags a day and little to no exercise, plus the stresses of living through a great depression, a world war, and the raising of eight kids.

But as times change, we must change too right?

Because let's face it, technology and the rise in social media has made it pretty hard for most of us to ignore health and wellness issues facing our world. For a start almost everyone wears an activity tracker these days, can monitor certain health stats and let's not even start on the role of Google as our greatest source of medical advice when we can't get a doctor's appointment.

The problem with the concept of wellness, however, is it is completely subjective.

Who gets to define what it really means, like on a day-to-day basis.

Plus, there is so much conflicting information out there about how to live a healthier and happier life. For some it means being a certain dress size and going to the gym three times a week while for others it means mental clarity, fresh air, and being able to still touch their toes.

I mean, the medical profession can't even make up their mind most of the time.

So who should we believe?

In January 2018, I was invited to take part in a BBC documentary called "Truth or Scare", a programme which investigates health claims to see if they hold up. This particular one was around the topic of "Can you be fit and fat?"

Initially the concept was they would get a slim but inactive person to do a range of exercises alongside me, and a GP would test who was the fittest.

I didn't know how this would pan out. I could have ended up with pie on my face as the nation witnessed car crash TV of me being completely embarrassed and proved wrong.

So, on a cold Saturday morning in east London, the TV crew and presenters assembled and the experiment began. I was marathon training at the time and the show was also filming at a local Parkrun about the positive impact of that initiative, so it made sense for me to run a 5K too. However, the lady who had been selected as the slim but inactive person didn't want to run 5K.

So she didn't run but I did, holding a video camera the whole way round the 5k circuit.

We were then asked to do a fitness test of step-ups on a box, to a metronome with our heart rate being measured both immediately after and a few minutes later to see how we recovered. We were also asked to do some star jumps for two minutes, to see how many we could do in a minute.

After all that, was it possible to tell who was fitter?

Well, the thing is it wasn't very scientific, any of it, and the GP's answer was that there wasn't a lot in it, which seemed like a lot of work to get such a mediocre result.

During my interview for the programme, I was asked what fitness meant to me. I said it was less about having wonderful cardio fitness or athletic ability and more about being fit for life, fit for the activities and lifestyle you want to lead.

An Olympic athlete is fit because they need to be to perform well at their sport. A middle-aged fisherman has a completely different type of fitness, which is about keeping up with the demands of the job - much like a stay-at-home mum might have to be able to run around after the kids and keep on top of housework, etc.

There is so much pressure by marketers and the media for us to look a certain way. Fitness influencers on Instagram, for example, are on the whole providing an unrealistic set of role models for the vast majority of us.

Recently I showed a photo of a list of the world's top fitness influencers as decided by *Forbes*, there was literally only one that the ladies in my coaching groups recognized and that was the BodyCoach, Joe Wicks.

Which makes you think who are these folks actually influencing?

Is it a realistic lifestyle or image they are portraying as the norm?

They have influence clearly, but are they experts?

Am I an expert?

Who even are the experts?

There is so much information and so much misinformation out there that it is difficult to know who to trust.

A doctor once told me I was too fat to run, and I have heard countless other stories of medical professionals giving weird advice based on their out-dated and often biased views on how women should live their lives.

However, one of the big problems is that we are too busy to do the research ourselves.

Most us want to be told exactly what to do.

It isn't as easy as that.

We have to be able to work things out for ourselves, because we are all so different.

Of course this doesn't mean ignoring the advice of our doctors...but there is nothing wrong in asking for a second opinion.

We have to be able to find our own sense of balance.

Your own equilibrium (check your dictionary...it's a great word)

Balance takes us back to the idea of the three-pronged stool I talked about earlier in the book. The idea of us having to focus on multiple things and it being a practice....and not something you are always going to get 100% right, all of the time.

The 3 legged stool of wellness

When I look back to the moments of real stress and turmoil in my life, it was always when one of the key themes of health, wealth or happiness were being neglected.

When a leg fell off so to speak.

And often when I had no purpose or direction.

Don't get me wrong, we can't always control all of this.

Sometimes legs fall off.

An accident can lead to bad health, being made redundant from a job can affect your wealth and a relationship breakdown, or a world event can affect your happiness.

These are somewhat out of your control.

But be aware of the importance of these factors on your sense of wellbeing for the things you can easily affect, and have strategies in place to keep each of these areas nicely topped up.

They don't have to be topped up equally but you can't just abandon any one element for the long-term, otherwise the other two are pretty useless.

Later in the book I will be asking you to think about your purpose, you will want to remember this image, and decide on whether keeping on top of the three pillars allows you to live out your purpose, or whether your purpose helps you to maintain the three pillars.

I will also be asking you to reflect on some of the most life-changing events and stories from your past, to look for clues and trends around any of these missing pillars. For example, a massive trend I have found is that ALWAYS, and I do mean ALWAYS...

Before a success in my life, always came an almighty fall.

Seriously, for every major life success I can trace back something shitty that I was dealing with at the time.

- Relationship breakdown
- Redundancy
- Family bereavement
- Falling out with a friend
- An illness or injury
- Media backlash

Sometimes, a life crisis like these is simply a wake-up call to something being unbalanced, and they serve as a brilliant wake up call to make the adjustments you need and want to make.

Before I break down the three main components and offer some tips for keeping these front of mind, I want you to think about whether you can see any connections between your own health, wealth and happiness.

For example,

- Does your health suffer every time something sad happens to you?
- Is your income affected by any health conditions you have?
- How easy is it to be happy when you are down to your last £10, or a big tax bill comes in?
- When you are stressed does your self-care go out the window?
- When you are happy/sad/stressed do you buy things you don't need?
- When you are in the throws of a new relationship, does your career suffer?

Let's have a further look at where these worlds collide.

Check and Challenge 28 – Are you still standing?

What do you already have in place in your life to keep this three-legged stool up standing? Which activities straddle two themes? And is there a weakest link?

We often feel like we don't have enough time, resources or energy to focus on more than one area of our life at a time, but often there are things we could do which hit all of your goals in one fail swoop.

It's what I like to call a Sweet Spot Pursuit

For me, my running is 100% a sweet spot pursuit.

It improves my health, both physical and mental, and because running is now a major part of my business, it literally pays for me to run. It 100% makes me happy because I am able to achieve goals and have also used it to make friends, travel and create new exciting experiences.

So clearly it is a win, win, win.

Conversely, writing can take me a little bit away from my sweet spot. I love to write, but often it impacts on my mental health because I stress and worry about being found out as a fraud or meeting deadlines, etc.

Plus, sitting at my desk for hours and hours is not good for my body. When I am deep into the writing process, I forget to eat, drink far too much tea, and often don't get enough sleep.

When we start to look at setting Big Fat Stupid Goals in Chapter 8, you will see how it makes sense to select goals which hit at least two out of the three pillars.

So let's spend a bit of time on each of these three pillars of wellbeing.

Health

He took one look at me and judged my health and my ability to run a marathon based purely on what I looked like, I don't think I've ever been so mad.

In my experience I don't feel like we ever really think about our health unless we are confronted with a worrying health issue or see the impact of someone close to us having a health scare of some sort.

For example, it takes me ages to bother going to my doctor with niggles or worries, because there are so many other competing priorities. How about you?

Do we ever really prioritise our health fully?

Plus, there is no real measure of good health really is there? When a 65-year-old answers the question "So are you generally in good health" they are answering from a completely different perspective to that of someone in their 30s. I mean, if I knew that the aches and pains I feel when I wake each morning would become my normal I'd never have believed you even just 10 years ago.

Let's not forget, the body is an incredible thing that we put through so much, don't we? Even when we don't really look after it too well.

Its ability to fix itself, repair, renew astounds me.

I can't tell you the amount of times I've been like: "Well, that's it, I'm fucked".

Whether that being a consistent bout of severe cold sores, excessive weight gain, pulling muscles, tearing ligaments, finding lumps in places they shouldn't be - and let's just skip over the potential liver damage I inflicted during my peak drinking years.

For many overweight women, it is hard to ignore that fact that health is often discussed in respect of our body size, as if it trumps all other wellbeing considerations.

The number one concern for fat people tends to be the impact of their weight on their physical health. Rarely do we care what the impact of being overweight (or other people's concern or even distain about your size) can have on your self-esteem and what this can mean for the quality of your life.

In this chapter I want to talk to you about my experiences of health, what I've learned over the years through working with thousands of women of all shapes and sizes, and how you can achieve a BIGGER more EXCITING, more FULFILLING life by looking after your health, even if that doesn't mean any weight loss.

Good health is not a given. It is not available to us all, no matter how hard some of us try. Some of us, for all manor of reasons, are born in to bodies with various states of disease, disability and into environments which just don't support good health. No level of blame or shame is going to change that, no matter how entitled those in better health believe they are to pass judgement. Unless you have lived in my shoes, back the fuck off, right!!!

Yes, the medical profession and public health bodies have made huge impact to our longevity, finding cures for terrible diseases, and I am eternally grateful to the NHS, but on an individual level, the only people who really have to live with our good or bad health is us...and maybe our nearest and dearest.

Yes, a doctor can make an assessment, but unless you want to change, nothing they say will make any difference. If you are being honest with yourself you know if you felt healthier at a size 18 or a size 20; you know whether that one dress size makes the difference between you being able to run for a bus or not; you know whether it impacts negatively on your mental health.

Some of the health issues we encounter through our life are not related to our weight at all, or perhaps are coincidental to us putting on weight. Only we can truly assess that journey, a GP who has 10 minutes to talk through your weight issues just simply doesn't have the capacity, and very few people get referred to reap psychological or cognitive support. So we have to find that elsewhere.

For example, I put on weight at university because I was drinking too much and eating an unbalance diet, but I don't think it impacted on my mental health or physical health in the slightest.

Whereas when I put weight on during pregnancy, it did affect my general health and wellbeing - in particular my confidence, but also my ability to just be agile and keep up with the demands of being a new mum.

Much of the health improvements I saw from losing weight were equally because I was just generally looking after myself better.

I have been healthier at a size 18 than what I was at a size 14/16 about a decade ago when I was abusing my body in a range of ways, including hard core dieting, while battling with depression. Being able to see this laid out in front of you in a visual way is quite a useful tool.

It helps you to spot your bullshit stories and notice any trends.

Having a flick through old photos is equally a great way of noticing things you may have missed otherwise. Like literally while writing this book I came a cross a stack of old photos and noticed one of me standing in the ocean in Mexico in a bikini with my sister back in 2008. My body doesn't actually look that different over a decade ago to what it does now, even though my negative narrative could have me believe otherwise.

Check & Challenge 29 - Do a health review timeline.

Take a piece of paper or draw this in your journal. Create two axis, one with the number of years you have been alive, do them in three-year blocks if you like, and then another axis with a scale of 0-5, and chart any peaks and troughs of your health.

If you are interested in how this correlates with any weight gain feel free to add a second line perhaps with a different coloured pen.

Draw an axis with a vertical line numbered 1-10 and a horizontal number 0 to your current age. Plot out the peaks and troughs in your health, taking into consideration physical and mental health, and things like short-term illnesses, broken bones, and anything else which impacted on your wellness. Feel free to make notes to remind yourself of these occurrences.

Here is an example of mine.

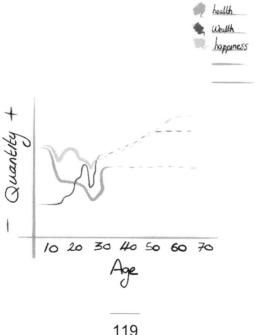

I would say I was in great health right the way up to about the age of 13. I had a varied diet, was very active, and was generally speaking a happy child (despite some turbulence during my parents' divorce).

I'd never had any major illnesses, never had much time off school, never had as much as a broken bone, no matter how hard I tried to get one.

At aged 13, I got a part-time job in my local Wimpy restaurant and my diet changed significantly. Not only was I eating burger meals twice a day each weekend, and as much fizzy drinks as I liked during my shifts, I also had cash to buy food I wanted, food which had been in short supply growing up.
I had also stopped going to dancing school, and was no longer engaged in sport at school or anywhere else. I was quite inactive in fact. It wasn't cool to play sport as a teenager, and nobody in my family had active hobbies so any kind of physical activity just stopped for a few years.

Puberty hit. Boobs arrived literally overnight and I developed hips. I remember feeling huge. Looking at photos now I can see I wasn't, but nobody around me told me otherwise and I started feeling self-conscious about my body and more generally about my appearance.

I felt FAT (how can that even be a feeling?) despite actually being of average size, if not a little tall for my age. Which should have been seen as an asset. I am thankful for my height now.

I wouldn't say I was in bad health during this point of my life, but I do believe it was the start of my difficult relationship with food, binge eating, not enjoying exercise and not being comfortable in my own skin.

I studied performing arts at sixth form school and college and had joined a local street dance crew with some friends, so the return to dance (even if not ballet and tap this time) saw my self-esteem and fitness improve.

Being more independent and away from the family home had a massive positive impact on my happiness levels too. As did the early encounters of teenage romance, and later an active and satisfactory sex life (sorry mum).

My choice of career was a blessing in disguise as I headed off to university to study Performing Arts where I had to participate in dance and physical theatre classes each week. However, my body was taking a bit of a battering by now with the discovery of alcohol, carb-heavy cheap food, and 16-hour shifts in – I kid you not - a local salad factory (oh the irony!)

I was clueless at this point about how to improve my health.

Hang on, who am I trying to kid.

I didn't care about my health, what I cared about was being FAT.

I was fatter than most of the girls on my course.

I was a size 18/20 by now and had no idea how to lose that weight. I was clueless about nutrition, didn't really have the funds to buy healthier foods, and despite being open to the idea of playing sport or joining a gym, I didn't have the time, money or any friends to do it with. I figured I would work on this when I returned to London after finishing my degree.

I'd go back to Weight Watchers with my mum, which would sort me out.

If I am being honest, fitness didn't really feature in my plans back then. If only I had found out about the impact of movement on my self-esteem and wellbeing back then, and of course had someone to do it with.

Growing up without any real role models in terms of sport and physical activity played a major part in this disconnection to it.

By the time I was overweight and out of shape in my early 20s, I had the belief that exercise was there now simply to help me shift the weight, I didn't believe it could be enjoyable and add to my life.

What joyful movement do you do?

I believe all movement should be joyful.

If you don't enjoy the gym you shouldn't go.

Just like how being forced to play hockey at school when you hated it was absolutely the worst advert for playing sport.

So what is Joyful Movement? Does it mean you have to be full of joy every moment of it?

Hell no, otherwise I'd never do anything.

Joyful Movement

- Where it fits in with your lifestyle
- Where it's not a chore
- Where you don't feel like you are exercising

- Where you do it irrespective of weight loss
- Where there are secondary benefits such as travel or social life
- Where it lights up your soul
- Where it makes you laugh
- Where you are happy to increase the effort occasionally
- Where you always feel better having done a session

There is a bit of a caveat here though...sometimes it takes a while for this joyfulness to come to you...especially if you are starting from scratch, or you already have aches and pains, or mobility issues.

Check and Challenge 30 – What exercise have you found joyful?

Write a list of physical or sporting activities that come under the joyful movement banner you have enjoyed in your life

Have a look at this list and ask yourself if there are any that you wish you still did? Why did you give them up? Are you physically able to do them? Even if you participated at a different level than you did previously. Is there a different exercise that has similar features?

Check and Challenge 31 – What joyful exercise would you like to try?

Come up with three new activities you would like to give a go over the next three months, and write down any resistance you might have to them. Things like...

- I don't know where this happens
- I have nobody to go with
- It's too expensive
- I don't know the rules
- I might be rubbish

Now have a look to see if any of this is bullshit? Are you talking yourself out of it before you even start?

Are you being creative enough?

Just don't make me run

Now it is well documented that I love running, that running literally saved my life...because it did. So I am not going to include running as an example of joyful movement because it goes without saying... and anyway I hate it as much as I love it... the joyful bit comes at the end of a session, and in the secondary benefits of it.

And I know some women just hate it as an activity.

Even I have my moments of hating it.

When you have been running for more than 10 years, with a number of those years the sport playing such a big part in your business, it is hard to stay motivated, and to not get bored of the same races, the same challenges, the same fitness gains.

After going up the various distances, travelling for races abroad, trying ultramarathons, obstacle courses and triathlons, I realised I needed a new challenge. I love running and all that comes with it, but after becoming a single parent running socially became quite difficult unless I paid for a babysitter, and even racing lost its appeal, I mean there are only so many weekends in a year right?

So I started looking for other fitness activities that would challenge me but fit better into my lifestyle. I'd love to say I found and embraced yoga, but I'm still working on that…I love the idea of being a Yogi…but I simply am not motivated enough to be consistent with it.

Eventually I found CrossFit.

About a year ago, I started to wonder how more intense training could impact on my fitness, body shape and running ability, and when I got the opportunity to try out my local CrossFit for a month I jumped at the chance.

What is CrossFit?

The official website describes it as: *"CrossFit is constantly varied functional movements performed at high intensity. All CrossFit workouts are based on functional movements, and these movements reflect the best aspects of gymnastics, weightlifting, running, rowing and more."*

Functional movements are the core movements of life. They move the largest loads the longest distances, and are ideal for maximizing the amount of work done in the shortest time.

In "Julie talk"…I would say CrossFit is a bloody good (but intense) work out which will challenge every aspect of your being as it's physical, mental and emotional.

A CrossFit box is the name for the venue they use and which are run by affiliate coaches. In my case this is Dan "Muzz" Aldridge and Martin "Flan" Flanagan, both ex-army blokes with more fitness qualifications to their names than they have tattoos between them - and they have lots of tattoos.

I initially started with their six-session beginner's course called Fundamentals so that I could learn all the essential moves under the careful instruction of the coaches before joining the main workouts.

CrossFit folks appear to speak a whole new language, which is actually quite easy to understand once you get to grips with it. It also makes you feel like you are part of a secret club

- **WOD** – Workout of the Day
- **AMRAP** – As many reps as possible within a given time frame
- **MetCon** – A Metabolic Conditioning Workout
- **Rx'd** – As prescribed; as written. WOD done without any adjustments or scaling down
- **FT** – For time. As in this is what you have to do, how quickly can you do it.

Then there are the different types of lifts to do with a barbell.

- **Thrusters**
- **Jerks**
- **Deadlifts**
- **Overhead Press**
- **Squats**

Sessions are written on the whiteboard and you do them at your own pace, it's not a competition with anyone else, although you do put your scores on the board afterwards. I have never felt like anyone is judging what I can do. I have also found that some people who look fitter, smaller, stronger than me are not always fitter, faster or stronger in everything.

We all have our own strengths.

But let's get things straight.

I am the fattest there. Let's be clear on that. I was when I started and I still am now.
Each time I turn up at CrossFit I know I am going to be pushed to my limits because the sessions are hard and I don't do anything else like this.

By showing up and taking part, you change the dynamic and perhaps even encourage other women to be brave enough to give it a go too because they won't be the only fat person there. CrossFit is bleeding hard work, but it teaches you how to push through mental barriers, build mental toughness and much, much more.

More than any other fitness activity I have ever tried, CrossFit has had the biggest impact on my overall health. I am stronger and more confident in my body's ability than I ever have been, and it has worked wonders for my confidence and mental health.

Exercise should impact on your physical AND mental health

If fitness isn't fun, then you should stop right?

Well, not sure if that is completely true.

Define fun for a start?

There are some people who just don't enjoy exercise.

What I would say is that when you look at the impact of movement on your mental health, it is hard to deny that it is a worthy activity to do.

Studies have shown that as little as one hour a week of low-to-moderate intensity exercise can help reduce symptoms of some mental health illnesses, and although research has yet to prove a cause-and-effect relationship between exercise and its ability to prevent the initial development of depression, it strongly suggests it.

Knowing that each time I exercise my brain is being flooded with endorphins and over and above any of the other benefits that exercise gives me, this is the true game changer for me.

When I go for more than four or five days without some intensive exercise I feel it in my body, I feel it in my mood. I start to feel low, I start to feel anxious, I start to lack confidence in myself.

Exercise reminds me that I am awesome, almost as if it shoots all these wonderful chemicals around my body as a wake up call to not give up on it.

When I say fitness saved my life, I actually mean that.

Can we talk about mental health for a bit?

A few years ago in the height of what I call my "Raving Years" a time where I had a lot of disposable income, and little direction or purpose, a string of things happened that led me into a spell of serious depression.

I have always been prone to moments of feeling down.

But this was something else.

I had recently split from a boyfriend of five years, I had started a new job that I hated, I had become a homeowner and money was really tight, and then my grandad died - not unexpectedly, but it was still very sad.

Each of those things in isolation would have been manageable, but collectively and with nobody really to support me through it, I felt terribly alone and couldn't cope.

I didn't really see it at first, as I was in this cycle of going out clubbing at the weekend, and then struggling through the week the best I could.

And then one weekend I literally could not get out of bed.

I had woke up with a massive cold sore, a monstrosity of a thing, and I couldn't motivate myself to get out to the chemist for some cream to relieve the pain at least.

But actually the cold sore was the least of my worries. Lying in that bed, my mind went to all kinds of dark places, as I questioned who would even notice if I wasn't there any more.

The spiral into complete darkness was drastic and fast.

I knew I needed help.

I knew that help wouldn't come from anyone I knew.

There wasn't a single person in my phone book who I felt I could reach out to.

And so I did something that I still can't believe I did .

I cycled to the local hospital.

And here's why.

I had no petrol in the car and I had lost my bank card the night before.

126

I would have had to queue up in the bank and that would have meant being seen.

If I cycled, I could take the backstreets and be there in 20 minutes without anyone seeing me.

And so that is what I did.

Only problem being, by the time I got to the walk-in centre, I felt great.

Well, maybe not great, but I felt a whole heap better.

When I spoke to the triage nurse, I explained about my cold sore, which was pretty horrific and painful, and then I burst into tears, simply because they were kind to me.

I saw a doctor.

He saw that this was not just about my cold sore. Clearly no amount of Zovirax was going to fix me.

The doctor suggested I spoke to a mental health practitioner who was on duty and I ran through how I had been feeling the last few weeks.

And before you knew it I was being diagnosed with clinical depression and chronic fatigue syndrome.

I had explained how even sitting at my desk at work, or travelling on the tube was making me exhausted.

I ended up having three months off work, two of which I was on antidepressants.

I never forgot the impact that bike ride had on how I was feeling though, the affect that exercise had on my mood. So a few weeks into being off work, I started swimming again, and then signed up for a 10K race.

It wasn't long before I was off the tablets all together and heading back to work.

That three-month period of my life when I was just about to hit 30 was probably the time of my life where I was in the worst health.

But I probably didn't look it...my social media feeds showed I was having the time of my life, and my relative youth was hiding all kinds of problems below the surface.

Check & Challenge 32 – Are you OK?

How is your mental health? Is it something you monitor? Do you ask for help when you need it? Do you know where to go for specialist help?

Check out the resources section at the back of this book

People can't see how you are doing on the inside, can they? And they won't know what's going on unless they take the time to ask you, or you volunteer that information, and not everyone is able to do that.

We will talk more about mental health under the happiness theme, but I just wanted to illustrate how exercise has always had this vital role in keeping me health both physically and mentally.

It took me a while to realise that.

But now I am super aware of it.

I schedule exercise almost as if it was medication.

For me it is.

In the back of this book you will find an emergency first aid kit, a resource to help you when you feel you are hitting or close to hitting rock bottom, or simply where you feel stuck.

Gentle physical activity will feature. It may not be 100% the solution, but it makes for a pretty good band aid while you sort out your shit or get further help.

Mindful Fuelling can work wonders too

I promised I wouldn't start telling you what to eat, so I won't.

However, I can't not talk about what we put in our mouths at all, can I?

Let's face it, food is often seen as the enemy. Seen as the thing that got us in this mess in the first place. The thing we have little or no control over.

We live in a context of food overwhelm - and lies.

Yes, we have a powerfully persuasive food industry which tells us complete untruths about what we should and shouldn't be eating, like the saturation of low fat, high sugar products, and packaging that imply that products are good for us, despite being full of chemicals.

We have equally powerful diet companies there to sell us a dream - of this better life we would enjoy if only we were smaller.

But here is a different view. Food too can be medicine. It doesn't need to be controlled.
We are not stupid. Most of us who have an interest in good health generally speaking know the foods that serve us and those that don't.

We have just stopped trusting ourselves.

We have stopped listening to our gut.

We don't pay attention to our hunger levels, and we are driven by other kinds of hunger, emotional, peer-led, societal pressures, stress...

And unlike other addictions we can't abstain. When we try to replace our diet with food-like substances our bodies know and they rebel. When we place our self "on a diet" we feel broken, hard done by, bullied.

But when we choose, when we really choose, and stick by that choice with absolute conviction, we are free.

When we become more mindful of what we are eating, where it has come from, what processes it has undertaken to get onto your plate or into your hand, it forces us to have a dialogue with our self about that choice.

How often have you consumed a food without even thinking about it, like our head is cut off from our gullet, as if it is not serving the purpose of nourishing us, where it is quite literally filling a gap?

Check & Challenge 33 – What is your preferred way of eating?

This is one of only two food-related exercises in this book, because I don't think food is the problem. I think self-awareness is.

I have found that this next exercise enables women to take back control and with one simple prompt, really contribute to a more balanced approach to fuelling.

In your journal write down what food you believe your body most needs to eat for:

Breakfast
Lunch
Dinner
And what fluids you need to intake

List five foods that you know do not agree with your physically
List five foods that do not agree with you psychologically (that perhaps make you binge, or anxious such as coffee/alcohol)

How would you feel if this was your normal way of eating? Where loosely speaking you stuck to this most of time, without feeling like you are "off-plan" when you choose differently?

Stick this list somewhere you can refer to it easily.

The other tool that is also simple-but-effective is a hunger scale.

Paul McKenna uses this in his hypnotherapy for weight loss; I just think it's a great tool to check in with yourself.

Check & Challenge 34 – How hungry are you?

Use this simple hunger chart to assess your physical hunger signals, and always follow this up with, am I hungry for anything else?

The Hunger Scale

1	2	3	4	5	6	7
Starving	Hungry	Peckish	Satisfied	Full	Stuffed	Feel Sick

A final word about health

We need to recognise that health is complex, and yes it has also become political.

It is not just our own business anymore.

As sad as that fact is.

Everyone thinks they get to have a say now.

The cost of healthcare, the impact of our health on our kids, the impact of our health on our longevity, on our environment - these are all issues we are having to face up to as humans.

We have to have a plan right?

We have to keep ourselves informed and be critical of everything we are told.

Maybe we want to make some adjustments, some changes and maybe we don't.

We get to choose.

If you are looking to use this Living a Bigger Life methodology to make some health improvements, you will be able to focus on this when we get to the goal setting and planning adventures section in Chapter 8.

The scale of that change is completely up to you.

In my view, there are two lines of thought when it comes to improving your health. You will know what is likely to work for you based on your track record of making changes and improvements to your life. For me, I find a combination of the two works really well for me, according to how much time I have available to me, and what else is going on in my life. These are:

Exponential Change – Change on a massive scale, with a lot of effort and in a shorter than expected time frame

Incremental Change – Small steps of change which over time get you closer to where you want to be.

A third option is to:

Do Nothing - To just go with the flow.

Rest assured, even when you do nothing something will still happen, and surely it's better to be proactive rather than reactive?

Looking at these options you will probably be drawn to one over the other, and it would be useful to ask yourself what that is about.

It is too easy to look at any health changes with our inbuilt "Diet Mentality".

Going all out in the first few days and then losing the will to live. Beating yourself up. Promising to start again on Monday. A constant yoyo pattern of hope followed by disappointment and regret, followed by hope again.

Conversely, some of us need a big scale mindset or lifestyle change to ensure we actually do something.

Be aware of how diet mentality fits into all areas of your wellbeing, for example are you throwing money at the "problem" and is it stopping you from being happy in your romantic relationships?

We need to move away from this all or nothing way of being, and see all of this stuff as a process, a way of being, a practice.

Wealth

It's not about how much money you have in the bank,
It's ultimately about what your wealth enables you to do

Hand up if you were brought up to believe that speaking about money is vulgar.

I was.

I can't ever really remember anyone ever having any kind of useful conversation with me about money if anything, my only memories of money talk came in the form of "we can't afford it" and "no you can't because I don't have the money".

In fact, when I told my mum I wanted to go to university, her exact words were:

"Well, who do you think is going to pay for that?"

I was always aware as a child that we were not rich.

I'm not sure I would have described myself as poor, but I know there were lots of things my friends had that I didn't, and I would have to wait my turn for even some of the essentials. Second-hand clothing was the norm, and making things stretch until payday.

I'm not sure if that money mindset ever truly leaves you.

I can remember quite early on in my life being determined to get a job so I could have my own money.

Being determined to be self-sufficient so that I didn't need anyone and so that I had choice.

Nobody really teaches you about financial management growing up, do they? Nobody prepares you for the decisions you will have to make and the options available to you.

I remember going off to uni and having to manage my finances. It was nightmare. I could never make my student loans last!

I racked up quite a lot of additional debt the summer after leaving university, simply because I had a cheque book - even though there was no money in my account.

I am much better with money these days, but I do often find myself falling back into the "oh I can't afford it" way of thinking, whether it is true or not.

How much would you pay for a cucumber?

I'm just going to say it outright....

I love cucumbers.

Before you start thinking all kinds of smutty things, I am talking about the long green vegetable often enjoyed in salads and posh sandwiches.

I love cucumber in salads, as crudités with hummus, on the side of curries, in yogurt dips. I just really like the fresh crunchy taste.

Chances are if you look in my fridge you will always find a cucumber or two.

However, this hasn't always been the case.

A few years ago, the price of cucumber went up from £0.50p to £1 - a 100% increase overnight.

I was in severe shock. A whole pound for a cucumber. Are they kidding?

I may or may not have been on a bit of a budget with my shopping at the time, but, either way, I decided it was an absolute outrage and I boycotted my favourite vegetable in protest, on the grounds that I simply couldn't afford the price increase.

Like seriously.

A few weeks into my protest though, I realised the only person who was being hurt by my protest was me, I missed my beloved cucumbers.

Plus...of course I could afford them, I was just choosing to tell myself that I couldn't.

The following day as I did my weekly shop, I splashed out and bought two.

Now, why do I tell you this story?

Don't worry, I am not sponsored by the Trade Association of Cucumbers, it's just that the slightly humorous episode really taught me a valuable lesson about my money mindset and my quickness to announce that things are out of my price range, even when they are not. It is a habit that I had had for the longest of time, judging all kinds of experiences and potential purchased based on this weird sense of affordability rather than value.

Since that time, which I now refer to as my "Cucumber Protest", I continue to monitor the rise and fall of prices in the salad aisle, but it rarely affects my buying decision. Heck sometimes I even opt for organic or those cute little snacking cucumbers, which are very pricey in comparison, and it never fails to remind me of how lucky I am that I can afford fresh fruit and vegetables at all.

Check & Challenge 34 – What can't you afford?

Make a list of all the mundane things you have not bought, or begrudge paying for even thought technically speaking you can afford them.

Is there something larger at play though when it comes to this idea of what we can and can't afford?

I think so.

When I started my fitness business, this question of affordability and value continued to pop up with potential clients. I would be promoting one of my very affordable (in my mind) online programmes to which some women would happily sign up, but some women would go out of their way to tell me that they couldn't afford it, which made me feel really bad.

I would receive emails with quite detailed explanations about current financial situations, and the fact that they "simply can't justify the expense". Now we are not talking massive amounts of money here, normally something in the region of £20 or so.

I know there are lots of people on low incomes, and for some people, £20 can feed their family for a few days, so this is not a dig at them. However, I do believe that some of these "I can't afford it" declarations were more about not seeing the value in what I was offering, or a brilliant cover up for what was really going on, which was...

"I want to do it, but I'm scared of doing it, what if I fail, let me just stay in my comfort zone and convince myself and everyone else of a reason not to do it. I know, I will use the cost as an excuse."

That there, my friends, is what we call a money block - and sadly a lot of women have them without even knowing about it.

I see it in the running world all the time, especially when it comes to women wanting to take part in races, overseas trips, retreats etc. The decision that they can't afford it is made super quick, without A. doing any real research, and B. taking any kind of action to find the money required or look at alternative ways of making it happen.

Try running, they say...

It's FREE, they say...

But what about the running shoes, I say

And the race entry?

And the technical running gear?

Have you seen the price of a decent sports bra these days?

And then there are the sports massages?

And the gels and supplements?

Oh and let's not forget the blister plasters!!!!!

Perhaps I need to take up naked yoga?

Does any of that sound familiar?

It always makes me laugh when people respond to the adverts for my paid-for programmes with comments such as:

"Oh, it's not FREE??? I thought running was supposed to be FREE?"

"Money is tight right now."

"I can download a c25k app for £1.49 why would I pay £25 for your eight-week programme?"

Yes... but will an app take the time to get to know you? Encourage you, ask you questions, give you virtual kick up the backside if you need one, help you make real life running friends, share more than 10 years experience, support you when it gets tough?

Erm nope!!

Yes, running is FREE if you are happy to run barefoot, without a sports bra (heaven forbid) and want to restrict yourself to running a two-mile loop around your home, and be content to do so without any professional help.

But for the rest of us...

Running is a multi-billion pound industry, and is one that continues to grow – as demonstrated by the increase in number and participation of concept races such as Pretty Muddy, Spartan & Tough Mudder, Disney Races, not to mention the big city marathons and the once-in-a-lifetime adventures. Sometimes it can feel like you have to remortgage your home to be able to take part.

It doesn't have to be that way though. There are lots of ways to do exciting running adventures on a budget AND there are lots of fun and easy ways to generate extra cash to help you make this an exciting part of your lifestyle. If you think international travel and adventure is only for the youngsters - or worse still, slim women - you are very much mistaken. I want to show you how you can do it.

Over the last few years, I have been undergoing a complete money mindset overhaul. A few years back, I had such a negative attitude to money and any ideas around adventure, I was like:

I can't afford that

Nah... traveling ain't for me

That's just for the youngsters

But in the past four years, for example, even as a single parent with a limited income, I have managed to travel to more than 15 countries as part of my running adventures and business journey, and I've taken part in heaps of exciting events around the UK too - and not just because I am a fitness blogger.

How someone views their financial situation often says a lot about how they view other areas of their life, as if they are living in lack.

What is lack mentality?

People with a lack mentality or mindset have often struggled with some type of fear of scarcity for as long as they can remember, it could be to do with money, but equally it could be to do with food, or love.

Believing that there is not enough to go round, or that it is not yours to have.

This fear may have come from a parent's behavior or attitude, or it may have come from real-life circumstances in where a lack of money caused a negative outcome.

A great example of this can be found with many of our grandparents who grew up in a post war world. After years of rationing, and learning not to be wasteful, mend and make do.

It rubbed off on their children, and on theirs.

I remember in my nan's later years, she would receive lovely gifts from her children and grandchildren and she would save them for best, wearing slippers until they were falling apart before starting on a new pair.

Now there is nothing wrong with being frugal, but when it impacts on your ability to enjoy life and find joy in the wealth you have amassed, then it can become a problem.

But what even is wealth?

Is it just about money?

The dictionary will tell us two versions,

"An abundance of valuable possessions or money."

and

"A plentiful supply of a particular desirable thing."

The second definition is much more useful for us in our quest for wellbeing.

Because this is not about being rich in the traditional sense of the word.

It is not about amassing lots of cash just for the sake of it.

This is not about the need for more, more, more.

Bigger, better, newer

You get to define what a wealthy, abundant, rich life looks like for you.

What if I feel ikky about money?

Lots of people do.

Many believe we should live simpler lives, and not be so wasteful, and that amassing wealth and assets is vulgar.

But what if the wealth you create can help others?

What if it gives you choices and options that make you a healthier, happier person, which in turn affects the people around you in a positive way?

What if having an abundance of what you need means there is lots left over for others and that you get to help redistribute it more fairly?

Check & Challenge 35 – Money memories

What money memories do you have from your childhood and early years as an adult that you feel may have affected how you view wealth now.

Here are some of mine

- Washing my aunty's car for £5 a go
- Babysitting for months on end so I could afford a Game Boy
- My first job in Wimpy being paid £1.50 per hour
- Walking for miles to see my dad and ask for pocket money, only to be told NO
- Crawling on our hands and knees by the side of the bed to raid my dad's jean pocket of his small change
- Swapping my younger siblings' pound coins for my small change because they didn't know the value of money
- Avoiding paying the train fair so I could buy lunch instead at college
- Getting out loans and store cards that I couldn't afford to pay back as a teenager
- My mobile phone getting cut off numerous times
- My younger brother stealing things I had worked hard to pay for
- Buying a second-hand car from someone in a pub car park, only to find out a few weeks later it was a stolen car
- Buying a brand new car and crashing it the following day
- Working freelance and getting paid all in one go and not knowing how to budget
- Being shocked at how much tax I would pay in my first fulltime job after uni
- Allowing boyfriends to pay for everything
- Paying for everything for other boyfriends

- Saving for two years to raise £14,000 for a deposit for my first home
- Worrying about money when I was made redundant
- Hating have to chase my ex for money for our daughter
- Never knowing if I could meet this month's mortgage payment
- Accepting help off someone I knew online when I had no money for food shopping

You see there is some juicy stuff in there.

For me the overwhelming message I got around money growing up was:

- There is not enough to go round
- You have to work hard to earn money
- Nothing is free
- You shouldn't accept help

And the biggest one for me is that of feast and famine.

Your stories might be completely different and that is OK too.

Now you might be thinking what has this all got to do with Living Bigger?

Well often we allow our finances to stop us living the life we want.

I will show you what I mean.

Check & Challenge 36 – Write down three life-changing things you would do if money was no object

For me they would be:

1. Always taking summers off work and going on adventures overseas with my daughter, Rose
2. Buying a house by the sea
3. Setting up a charity that supports women and girls to talk more effectively about their bodies.

I now believe that some of these things will be available to me.

Not because I expect to become a millionaire anytime soon (but hey let's not write it off), but because I have a much clearer idea of what I want, my business and life is positioned around making these come true.

I also know I can do variations of these things on a smaller scale with or without money. I am not using the lack of funds to stop me.

Check & Challenge 37 – Using money as an excuse

Can you list five occasions where you have used lack of money or the expense of something as an excuse not to participate. Did you regret it afterwards? Were there other reasons at play? Would it have been better to be honest about the real reason?

Here are some of mine from past and present

1. Not joining a gym – *Real reason, I wasn't ready to commit*
2. Not buying clothes after my pregnancy – *I didn't want to be visible*
3. Hire a business coach – *I was worried I wouldn't do the work*
4. Hire staff – *I am worried they won't do a good job*
5. Not moving home – *I am scared to move out of London*

Surely there is a link between money and health too

It doesn't take a genius to make the connection between the eating of crap food and having little money in your purse does it? You only have to think about how you felt as a child with 50 pence in your pocket, it was all about how much you could get with your money. What gave you the biggest high for the smallest amount of spend - so bring on 20p panda pops, 10p space raiders and 20p of penny sweets.

Or was that just my experience of childhood?

When I look back at my journey with food I can say without a shadow of doubt that I grew up with an overwhelming sense of scarcity. Being one of six children there wasn't a lot of spare money around, and although we rarely went hungry it was always a case of "get in quick before someone else does". We never had a biscuit tin, the fruit bowl could be demolished in a matter of days and eating out as a family was a rare occasion often limited to trips to the seaside or family holidays, with regular tantrums about having to share a bag of chips when things were really tight.

I don't think those feelings of food poverty ever leave, and as soon as I was able to earn my own money, food was often a way that I treated myself, especially when I was away at university with nobody looking over my shoulder to see how much veg I was eating.

A report from the National Statistics office notes:

"Obesity is linked to social class, being more common among those in the routine or semi-routine occupational groups than the managerial and professional groups. The link is stronger among women. In 2001, 30 per cent of women in routine occupations were classified as obese compared with 16 per cent in higher managerial and professional occupations."

Researchers at the Department of Social Medicine at Bristol University have also concluded that:
"...social origins may have a long term impact on obesity. Whether this operates through the early establishment of behavioural patterns, such as diet and exercise, or through metabolic changes associated with early deprivation, is still to be determined."

How do we upgrade our money mindset though?

Over the last few years I have been working with a Money Mindset coach called Denise Duffield Thomas and through her work have been identifying my self-limiting beliefs, looking back into my past to see where some of my money issues came from, and most importantly upgrading my life in tiny little increments so that I begin to start valuing myself properly...buying new underwear for example (Too much information??)

When it comes to food, I have noticed because of this I have been shopping differently and therefore eating differently too. I am no longer bulk-buying, or buying multipacks, I am instead thinking about what foods I really want and which are going to nourish me. It's about telling myself that this is what my body deserves.

Whereas before I might wince at the price of gluten-free bread (£3) I now remind myself that normal bread makes me feel bloated, and because I freeze the bread and use it sparingly I am actually spending less on bread overall...and more importantly doing what is right for my health and sense of wellbeing.

But it's not just food that we are talking about here, there is also the matter of paying for exercise or support around nutrition...or even trips to the physio for a massage.

I used to tell myself that I couldn't afford a gym membership or pay for a personal trainer and looking back I realise this was not about how much disposable cash I had, but rather how much I valued my health and the things I would rather spend my money on...think £7 mascaras, £6 magazines, lunches out, partying!!!!

Now I know for many people in the UK, and around the world money is tight. I wouldn't be as flippant as to say if you really wanted to do something you would find the money, but I think we need to start being honest with ourselves about the situation.

Rather than falling back on the default "I can't afford it" I think we need to be saying "I am choosing not to at this point in time" or "I am not ready to make that investment yet" and changing that self limiting belief and lack mindset.

There is always a way. Always. And if that statement annoys or frustrates you, journal on why it does, and ask yourself if you are being really open to the idea of new possibilities. If your current income doesn't cover your living costs...someone could gift you the thing you need.

We can agree to disagree on the money front because women do have different income levels and access to disposable cash, but we all have the same amount of time in a day. So many women tell me they want to get fit but can't find the time, yet the same women happily tell me what's going on in their favourite soap opera or that they spent the weekend walking around the shops looking for shoes to match their latest handbag.

It's all about choice.

Isn't it selfish to spend money on yourself?

I'm not sure where this attitude to money comes from with women?

According to Ruth Hayden, the author of "For Richer, Not Poorer" women have been taught to purchase for lifestyle and children, while men have been taught to invest in items that hold value. She says,

"We're becoming more interested learners of money, but we have not shown much difference in the *doing* part. And it's the *doing* part that creates financial security for us."

I read somewhere that men spend significantly less of their disposable income on others, than women who happily spend the lions share of theirs on those they love, in the form of gifts, treats, kids activities, charity donations and loans to friends in need.

What about stuff just for you?

Do we not deserve to invest in ourselves however we choose?

What if you could spend money guilt-free on adventure, learning, fun and joy?

Check & Challenge 38 – Create a Living Bigger Fund

What if you were able to earmark some money each month that was just for you? You wouldn't have to save a lot. You could start with £10 or £20 per month, and decide whether to use it each week, month or year.

How great would it be to be able to experience new things, reach for your goals, focus on your health and happiness in the knowledge that you already have the funds available to you?

For example, one of the ladies in my Living a Bigger Life programme has a 'fun fund' with her mum and sister. Each month, they each put £20 into a dedicated bank account, and once it has grown into a suitable amount of money, they spend it on having quality time together. Their Fun Fund has paid for Michelin-starred meals, spa weekends, trips to theatre and European travel – all experiences they would have been unable to afford had they needed to find the money in one lump sum.

The haves and the have nots

I used to feel really uncomfortable around rich people. If ever I met someone through work who clearly was on a more substantial income that me or from a different social class I would feel a bit on edge, like I was being judged or looked down on.

This will have come from social conditioning, with comments such as:

"Rich people are different to us"
"Rich people are rude/mean/greedy/ruthless"

But what I have found to be true is that people are just people, some rich people are lovely, just like some are arseholes.

Whether you have money or not is kind of irrelevant.

Creating more wealth just makes you more of what you already are in my view. We have all seen the stories of lottery winners spending like crazy, buying trashy-looking things and then ending up with nothing again.

But equally we have seen good people make a lot of money through ethical businesses who go on to do life-changing work with their profits.

Ways of attracting more wealth

Is it simply about earning more money though?

I don't think so.

As I alluded to earlier we were reasonably poor growing up, but come on let's face it I always had a roof over our head, food in our bellies and had a decent education. We were not poor by comparison to people in other circumstances.

This is the thing though, just like health and happiness, wealth is not a matter of "just because I have more than some, it's not OK for me to want more". Being aware of other people's financial experiences doesn't negate your situation but of course it does give you some perspective.

At the height of my money worries, after becoming a single parent with a mortgage to pay and no job, when I found myself really down, with no food in the cupboard and the mortgage bill getting ever closer, I would force myself to look around at what I did have, and not allow myself to feel so helpless.

I had come from nothing before. I could do it again.

The magic of gratitude

I started practicing gratitude around three years ago.

It is a very powerful tool for being more mindful of the abundance you have already, and in terms of welcoming even more into your life without having a weird, desperate nature all the time.

For example, after my partner left, I wanted to get a new bed. It was an old bed, I'd had it for more than 10 years, and it was always supposed to be temporary as it was uncomfortable. Energetically it felt weird having it too (I'm strange like that). But I didn't have the money for such luxuries.

I started thinking about how lucky I was to have a bed at all.

I started making more of an effort to keep my room tidy, and to make my bed. I bought some new bedding...felt gratitude for that. A few months later I was able to buy a new mattress on credit, and I made sure I practiced gratitude on that. And then a few months after that a new bedstead.

The gratitude piece was important. I had to appreciate what I already had before I could expect anything better to show up. This can be used for your health and happiness too. We are so quick to talk and think about all the bad stuff in our lives, leaving little room to celebrate the good.

Check & Challenge 39 – The habit of gratitude

Every night before I go to sleep I think of three things I am grateful for.

I have been doing this religiously for the past three years and it has absolutely changed my stinking thinking into something more positive.

When I get out of bed each morning, I say "Thank you, Thank You" as each foot hits the floor - a reminder that I am alive and should be appreciative of the opportunity I have ahead of me.

Create a gratitude habit and try it for 21 days straight.

Remember to journal and see what comes up for you.

What else of value do you have in your life that you are not noticing?

I learned this technique from Denise Duffield Thomas and will be forever grateful.

This is all about being able to track what comes into you each and every day both in terms of hard cash, but also valuable things with a financial value.

You can do it on a simple spreadsheet or on an app.

I started doing this religiously in the last quarter of 2015. What I noticed was I wasn't as poor as I thought I was, and actually had a lot to be thankful for, especially in terms of the amount of FREE stuff I received.

We will talk about this more in Chapter 8 when we start literally conjuring up the stuff you want out of thin air (bear with me on this…it really does work)

As a fitness blogger I have always been great attracting things that had value, starting with low-cost items and then these increasing in value as I got more popular. What I wasn't doing was acknowledging the joy that these things brought.

- Race entry £30
- Luxury Backpack £60
- Pair of trainers £90

- Bluetooth Headphones £120
- Two weeks supply of pre-prepared healthy meals £160
- Autumn collection from new plus-size clothes company £400
- Upgraded to first class when flying back from a conference in Florida £600
- All expenses trip to Geneva £800+
- Equipment, sports watch and trip to do Paris Triathlon £2000+
- All expenses trip to TelAviv £1000+
- All expenses trip with three members of my family to Euro Disney £2500+
- All expenses family trip to Wales £1200+

This is just a small example of some of the value I had attracted into my life.

I can't actually pay my mortgage with any of this, but they are a great perk of the job and have given me enormous comfort, and in the early days an absolute relief from some quite challenging times.

I estimate that in the five years I have been in business I have attracted over £100,000 in value. Now that is not to be sniffed at.

Just imagine what £100,000 of value feels like to someone rebuilding their life?

Check & Challenge 40 – Noticing what comes in

To make sure I don't get complacent, I say a small thank you to each and every amount of money that comes into me. In the early days of my business this was literally amounts of £10, but I would be thankful as if they were £100 or £1000.

My business (like many these days) is built on these micro-payments, because I always try to make my programmes as affordable as possible.

When launching a new programme, I would do a happy dance as the PayPal notifications popped up on my phone. Not because I am necessarily money-driven, but more because each and every one of those transactions represented a woman who was coming to be for support. Each and every one of those transactions represented another step to financial freedom.

Money doesn't buy happiness? But it sure as hell gives you choices, freedom, security that you often don't have when you have no money.

A final word about women and their money blocks

Not everyone wants to talk about money.

Not everyone feels comfortable even thinking about their finances.

People will be triggered by it

People will be triggered by you making more of it.
Over the years I have had to really look at my views on money, because running a business as transparent as mine forced me to.

I get emails from women all the time asking me for FREE stuff.

I used to always give heaps of places away.

But then I got wise to it.

Yes, women have financial hardship, but I have also had financial hardship and I am not running a charity.

People have to acknowledge there is always an exchange of value. Nothing in life is FREE, even when I was receiving all that so-called FREE stuff, the companies were receiving something in return. A blog post, social media profile, brand association.

What I noticed as a rule was less than 10% of women who I gave free spaces on my online training courses would complete the programmes anyway.

What I offer now instead are great payment options, a FREE 10-day "make money for your adventures" mini-course, and I am always up for discussing ways of making it happen.

To truly invest in your health and happiness, you have to truly invest in yourself.

This doesn't always mean throwing money at your problems, but there has to be something you are willing to give.

Be that

- Time
- Money
- Focus

Happiness

Happiness is something that takes practice,
cos it is so much easier to be a miserable bastard.

Every Saturday morning, from the age of three and a half, to the age of 11 and a half, I went to Yvonne Dearman's Stage School in East Ham. They were the happiest years of my life.

Maybe it was the friendships I made, maybe it was the fact I was doing something I was pretty good at, or maybe it was just the sequined costumes and the smell of hairspray that did it for me.

Each year I would take part in our annual dance show, where 200 or so kids from our dance school, aged from three right the way up to women in their 60s would show off what they had been working on all year.

It was brilliant, especially watching the routines of the older girls, who of course I wanted to be just like.

It was great seeing dance routines from girls who were not in your age category, and who rehearsed on different days and times. It was a celebration of the joy we all felt from being able to move our bodies.

Two routines will always stick out for me, and for two different reasons.

My sister Jennie was a shy girl, and dancing really brought her out of herself. She did a dance routine to the song Baby Elephant Walk a song written in 1961 by Henry Mancini for the 1962 film, Hatari.

The tune was so damn catchy, so it's hardly any wonder it earned Mancini a Grammy Award for Best Instrumental Arrangement that year. I doubt I will ever forget how it goes until the day I die.

Anyway the dance routine was your typical dancing school jazz routine affair - very simple, but 20 or so eight year olds dancing in formation, on bare feet tip toes, skipping, galloping, holding hands, and smiling.

I will never forget the costumes.

Yellow catsuits with black fringing along the neckline.

The routine was so popular that it kept being revived for a few years, until the costumes didn't fit anymore. I often wonder where all of those girls are now, and how horrified they would be at the thought of wearing such a revealing outfit.

The second routine was a massive tap dancing number with literally 40 five and six year olds, each with their own small plastic chair.

How Yvonne pulled this off I will never know.

Being able to direct my own five-year-old to follow simple instructions proves difficult at the best of times, so to choreograph a whole class full was something short of a miracle.

The reason I remember this routine is because of the hilarity of kids getting it wrong, and going round the chairs in opposite directions, but also the song choice.

The song was "Happiness", known in the UK as the theme tune of comedian Ken Dodd who did a recording of it in 1964.

The lyrics are again etched into my mind for eternal reference.

Happiness, happiness, the greatest gift that I possess
I thank the Lord I've been blessed
With more than my share of happiness

To me this world is a wonderful place
And I'm the luckiest human in the whole human race
I've got no silver and I've got no gold
But I've got happiness in my soul

Happiness to me is an ocean tide
Or a sunset fading on a mountain side
A big old heaven full of stars up above
When I'm in the arms of the one I love

Happiness, happiness, the greatest gift that I possess
I thank the Lord that I've been blessed
With more than my share of happiness

I dare you to listen to this and not experience a slight shift in mood.

I dare you to listen to this on a bleak day, and not imagine those naive, innocent children in their sparkly dresses (smart trousers, shirt and bow ties for the few boys) and clean white tap shoes and not smile.

That's the thing about kids, they know what it is to express total joy? They know how to create it, they know how to share it, they know how to express it. We need to get some of that back don't we?

Check and Challenge 41 – What brings you joy?

Make a list of 10 things that bring you pure unadulterated joy?

Mine would be (in no particular order)

1. Clean bedding
2. Dancing
3. Watching stand-up comedy
4. Snogging
5. Swimming at night in the sea
6. Being at the beach
7. Cuddles with Rose
8. Being with my siblings when they are on good form
9. Travel
10. Adventure

A very simple way of making space for this joy is to work out the things which bring the opposite, so write a second list which outlines the things which bring you absolutely no joy - or further still have a negative effect on the joy in your life.

Mine would be:

1. Washing up
2. Ironing and sorting clothes
3. Email management
4. Watching Jeremy Kyle or other such crap on TV
5. Moany people on Facebook
6. Making sales calls
7. Rude people
8. Packing and unpacking suitcases
9. Dealing with cold calls
10. Sitting in traffic

So surely if we worked to eliminate or perhaps even reduce these from our life, we would get closer to our goal of happiness or a life full of joy.

Because, Happiness is the goal right?

But nobody tells you as a child that the goal in life is happiness do they?

Well nobody did in my family.

I wish they had of.

Even now I have to remind myself that happiness is a worthwhile pursuit, even if it is a little intangible to measure.

Be happy Julie, just be happy.

I grew up with the underlying message that the thing that you should strive for is to just not be shit at life. To do your best, hope for the best, and not get completely fucked over by the best of the best.

I kid you not.

Don't get me wrong I had a happy childhood. I have great memories of long summer holidays spent playing with my siblings and cousins, trips to the seaside and the occasional theme park, and being able to roam the local streets playing run outs and building camps.

We didn't have much in terms of material things and trips abroad were not really a thing once there were more than two of us. But we had each other, and were never short of something to do to entertain us.

There was a bit of an undercurrent of moaning though...you know that general consensus that life was a bit shit and there was nothing we could do about it.

My grandad was a wonderful moaner.

I often liken him to one of comedian Harry Enfield's characters where he is always like:

"You don't want to do it like that, you want to do it like that."

And if my nan resembled anyone it would be Catherine Tate's famous nan character:

"What a bleedin liberty?"

Now of course I loved them dearly, and in fairness they were not like those characters at all, I think it was just a sign of the lives they had lived.

Who has time to work on happiness when you have eight kids to cook and clean for, or provide for?

The thing is we know more now about the impact of happiness on our health, we are more aware of techniques to increase our happiness. Come on, let's face it, we have more freedoms than the folk of my nan and granddad's generation ever did.

We have more to be happy about really, don't we?

Even if they do reminisce on the good ole days.

So let's talk for a bit about being Fat and Happy

Have you noticed that these two terms are often discussed together?

There is the:

"Oh she's fat but she's happy" comments.

There are the:

"Funny fat friend" stereotypes, perpetuated greatly by TV and movies

And let's not forget the alternative viewpoint of:

"She must be really unhappy to be that size"

Is there a correlation?

I once posed the question in my journal.

"Am I unhappy because I am FAT or am I FAT because I am unhappy?"

It is still something I ponder on.

Initially I think I used food emotionally when I was unhappy.

Now I am not so sure.

Am I happy despite my fatness?

Am I happy because of it?

Does it not feature at all in how I measure my happiness?

What I have realised is, that for me my health is paramount and that yoyo dieting made me unwell. The mental strain of being hopeful and then disappointed as another regime failed to work for me was too much to bear.

For as long as I saw FAT as the thing stopping me from being happy, I wasn't looking at any of the other contributing factors in my life.

I have tried not to be FAT. I really have.

Exercise, healthy eating, therapy... I have thrown all kinds of resources its way.

However, I may always be this size.

I have made my peace with that.

I realised after having my daughter and having a good couple of years of being desperately unhappy, that I had to focus on things other than becoming physically smaller. Things that would see a better success rate.

I didn't need to be smaller, but I did NEED to be happier.

And I had to take my own needs more seriously.

The irony being, I needed to work out what it was I actually needed.

What do you need?

Abraham Maslow's hierarchy of needs is a well-known motivational theory in psychology comprising a five-tier model of human needs, often depicted as hierarchical levels within a pyramid.

Needs lower down in the hierarchy must be satisfied before individuals can attend to needs higher up.

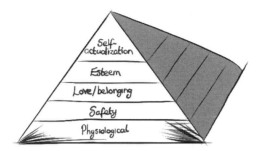

I am no psychologist and I am not going to argue with the great man himself, but is it that straight cut? As humans, are all of our needs exactly the same, or are these just guiding principles?

Some people for example like to be alone, and don't require any form of interaction with others. Some of the happiest people of all live in isolation or in relative solitude, Tibetan monks for example.

Some people live in pretty unsafe environments their whole life and still manage to function pretty well.

What I do like about these models though is it does make us think and even acknowledge that as humans we have needs.

As women we NEED reminding of that fact.

We are humans. Yet sometimes our family pets get more of their needs attended to than we do.

Surely that can't be right?

Check & Challenge 42 – What are the NEED ingredients for your happiness

We all have specific needs and wants for happiness, don't we? What are your unique ingredients for happiness? Do you even know? Have a think about the things you need/want in your life to enable more happiness.

Write them down in your journal, and then see if you can group them into four or five headings, before listing them in order of priority.

For me, what happiness really boils down to are four key things.

1. **Connection**

2. **Order**

3. **Achievement**

4. **Laughter**

Turns out these create a bit of an acronym (did you spot it?)...I know ACRONYMS can be a bit wanky in books...but hey I saw it as I typed it out and I could hardly ignore it.

Especially as it gives me such a cheesy strapline.

COAL – The fuel needed to fire your happiness furnace.

So let me share with you why this works for me.

1. **Human Connection**

Life can be a bit lonely, can't it?

We all want to feel loved and understood, don't we? And to have a wide circle of friends to be there through the good and bad.

But for many of us, life just hasn't panned out like that.

So many of us find ourselves socially isolated, and longing for more human connection.

Did you know that loneliness can be as damaging to your health as smoking?

Having a life with little social interaction is sadly not only a problem for the elderly but for many of us. The impact it has on our bodies is thought to be equivalent to smoking over a dozen cigarettes a day according to report commissioned by the UK government.

The report revealed a staggering nine million people in the UK are suffering from loneliness, and this is having a tangible and physical impact on us all with rising depression and suicide rates. A lack of mental stimulation also means that lonely people are 64 per cent more likely to develop dementia, which is a double whammy because sadly women often become the carers for elderly relatives adding even more strain.

It may come as a shock to you but I often feel lonely.

I live a very fulfilling life, but as a single parent who hasn't dated in what feels like decades, it feels odd to not have someone special to share my life with.

I have a wonderful bond with my daughter who I love spending time with, but you can hardly talk late into the night about your deepest life goals and desires with a five-year-old can you?

Sometimes I simply long for adult company.

As an entrepreneur this loneliness is extended as I spend huge chunks of my time alone in my office. I literally have thousands of digital friends and connections who I communicate with every day, but there is nothing better than being in the same physical space as the people you love or even people who you are yet to work out if you like.

Despite having some wonderful friends and a large family, the logistics of modern day life combined with the unconventional life I have chosen for myself, it means I don't always feel as connected as I could do.

So I have to keep a check on this, and construct a life of human interaction, just like I curate other aspects of my life.

- I have business buddies, and am part of in person and virtual mastermind groups
- I speak regularly to a close circle of friends and family
- I plan holidays, and meet-ups
- I attend conferences and events
- I reach out when I am feeling particularly lonely (although this one still remains the hardest thing to do)

The worst thing I can do is feel sorry for myself and do nothing.

I can be in my own company quite happily, but sometimes I realise that I have been doing so for unhealthy periods of time...and I have to be more sociable.

I feel most energised in the company of other people, so I'd be a fool not to instigate that as often as I can.

Check and Challenge 43 – Arrange some people dates

Look at the month ahead and schedule some dates with your favourite people. Bonus points if this is with people you have lost touch with or rarely get to see.

2. Order

I like to be in control.

I am quite disorganised by nature, even though I long for a more organised life.

I like to have a plan, even if I don't stick to it.

I need to know that I am following a process and there is method to my madness.

You can normally tell the extent of how balanced my life is by three things in my home:

- My hallway sideboard
- My dinner table
- My desk

These are a pretty good visual indicator of how life is working out for me.

If they are disorganised and a mess, chances are I am too.

For context, I live in a two-bedroom flat from which I run my business. What was once a clutter-free apartment with space for a lodger is now a cramped living space for a multi-passionate entrepreneur, her five-year-old gymnastic loving daughter and two rather neglected gold fish.

I have to have order in my home otherwise I couldn't function.

When I was pregnant with Rose, I had a massive clear out and turned my spare room into her nursery. While doing this I commissioned a furniture company to come in and fit additional storage on both sides of the room, knowing that we would fast run out of space.

In my two-bed apartment some how I manage to store:

- Two bikes
- Heaps of fitness equipment & kit
- Camping equipment

- Two marquees
- Xmas tree and decorations
- Sewing, knitting and crafting items
- Business records and files
- A fully functioning video recording studio
- Branded banners and pop ups
- Freebies sent by brands

Plus all of the paraphernalia that comes with having a five-year-old daughter

- Pushchairs
- Roller skates
- Scooters
- A billion books
- Arts and crafts materials galore
- Dolls, dolls and more dolls
- Dressing up kit
- Musical instruments

In order to keep any kind of order in my home, I have these things in place:

1. A weekly cleaner
2. A monthly decluttering day

Keeping your physical space in a state of order will work wonders on your happiness levels.

Check and Challenge 44 – Decluttering made easy

First, read *The Life-Changing Magic of Tidying* by Marie Kondo. This book is genius, and will revolutionise the way you view your stuff and your life FOREVER.

Then make a list of 10 areas of your life that need decluttering, and work on one a week, or a fortnight - whatever suits your schedule.

But then - and this is the way to really keep on top of things - deploy the 10 things to trash method, a method which quite literally means every single day you find 10 items that you no longer need or want and remove them from your home/life.

Do not move them from room to room in the hope you will find them a new home. Remove them completely from your living space. I try to recycle and donate to charity etc where possible as I don't like to see waste. It is a great wake up call in terms of how much rubbish we accumulate and how little we actually need.

The way I see it, the less stuff we have, the more space we have to really live.

Often as women we complain about not having enough time to do the things we want. Not having enough time to prioritise our health and happiness, not having enough me time.

Sometimes this 100% is the case, and the only option is to de-clutter and remove some of the load. But too often what I see is women who just haven't given their lives and the way they lead them enough consideration.

These women literally allow all sorts of crap into their lives and then wonder why they feel overwhelmed.

Marie Kondo encourages us to ask ourselves a wonderful question in relation to almost EVERYTHING in our lives.
"Does this spark joy?"

It is a great way of working out what needs to be de-cluttered or upgraded in your life, so that you can free up time and space in your life for things that do.

3. Achievement

I am motivated by praise.

I always have been.

I think deep down those messages of not being good enough and wanting to get more love and attention are still with me. So being able to achieve things that others don't always achieve in life is a big driving factor for me.

But actually it's more than this.

Not only am I motivated by other people praising me for my accomplishments, I just generally feel good when I can see I am making progress. Where I can track improvements. Where I can see that the effort I have put in is reaping rewards.

I am goal-orientated.

I love nothing more than ticking off a To Do list.

Or completing a training session as outlined on a training plan.

Also, I love being able to prove people wrong.

I often say people are motivated by two things:

Fame or Shame

I would say I am motivated a little by both.

The celebrity status of achieving something great, even if it is just your friends and family who think you are a super star after completing a Tough Mudder.

And, the motivating factor of "I'd better not quit because I told everyone I was doing this thing, and how embarrassing would it be if I didn't do it".

I am interested in how far I can take things.

I am interested in the process, and the commitment required to achieve great things.

I am interested in how we inspire others to follow in our wake

I am interested in how we evolve as the human race

And the role I could play in that - even in a tiny way.

You know the problem with having the desire to achieve great things?

Too often we are actually afraid of success. We are afraid of what it would mean to be successful. The attention it would attract. The haters that might surface. The impact it would have on our relationships. The pressure we would be under to continue in our greatness.

Once you let go of those fears, and accept that there is greatness in you and that you would be doing the world a disservice to not fulfil your potential, then you can get on and actually start enjoying the journey.

Check & Challenge 45 – 10 amazing things in a day

Make a list of 10 things you could achieve in just one day, if you focussed 100% on just those things. Bonus points if you share that list with loved ones or the world for added accountability.

These can be mundane things like change the bedding, clean the fish tank, file my tax return, or they can be more exciting things such as get my nails done, buy some flowers, have a massage.

Or connected to one of your bigger goals, they could be productive things such as writing a blog to share on LinkedIn raising your profile, or fixing meetings with potential new clients.

The idea is to batch these, and just get them done.

4. Laughter

Laughter is great for the soul.

When was the last time you laughed?

Laughed until you cried?

Laughed until you wet yourself?

I'm not talking a smirk, a chuckle, a brief moment of laughter; I am talking about the type of laughter that has you waking up the next day with abdominal pains. Belly laughter.

How often do you have something to laugh about?

How often do you let it out?

One of the people that always makes me laugh is my sister, Jennie. All of my siblings make me laugh, they are indeed a funny bunch, but my sister Jennie knows me so well, and we have some incredible shared experiences to laugh about.

We just get each other.

I remember a few years she texted me to say she was feeling a bit down. She had recently split with her partner and was living temporarily back at the family home - enough to make anyone a bit depressed right?

She was stuck.

She just had to sit it out and wait for things to settle down before making her next step. She wasn't destitute; she had a roof over her head and food in the cupboards, and a job and a car. But I guess she was just processing all the stuff that had gone on over the last few years and was feeling a little sad.

At first I didn't know what to do or say, I wasn't in the best of places either to be fair, but then I had an idea. So I sent her a string of texts, that went like this...

"Wanna play a game"

"What?

"To cheer you up, wanna play a game"

"Yeah go on"

"List the three funniest things that ever happened to you"

"What?"

"Just do it"

"OK"

And that's when she started.

Now for obvious reasons I'm not going to expose her in this book, but let's just say that some of her stories were hilarious. I started sharing mine. And then we started reminiscing over some of our shared experiences, and that was when the fun really started.

We were laughing literally until we couldn't breathe - and all of this over text message.

When my partner came in, he thought something was wrong.

And it was so funny I couldn't even explain to him why I was laughing.

That laughter session was like tonic.

A study in Norway found that people with a strong sense of humor outlived those who don't laugh as much. The difference was particularly notable for those battling cancer.

As the saying goes, "If I didn't laugh, I would cry."

In fairness though, I am a big fan of having a bit of a cry every now and again too...its an incredible release.

Whenever I feel low, I know a good laughter session is needed, and so I make it happen either by:

- Watching a funny movie
- Watching stand-up comedy
- Spending time with my friends/siblings

And get this one...

- Writing my own stand-up material

163

In 2016, I agreed to take part in a comedy night at a conference I attend every year, I had never done stand up before. I was terrified. But something about facing that level of fear light me up.

The process of looking at all the funny stuff that had happened in my life was very therapeutic, being able to then exaggerate and look for the punch line made it even better.

I actually went on to win a best newcomer at a local comedy club, smashed my gig at the conference, and was even invited up onto the stage at a comedy venue in Cape Town.

There is nothing more joyous than being able to make other people laugh

Check and Challenge 46 – Laughter therapy

Make it a goal to help someone else find laughter every day. Find something to laugh at or someone to laugh with. Think about the style of comedy that really gets you, and seek it out. YouTube is awash with FREE material.

Knowing what makes you tick, what makes you happy and what makes you sad. What makes you anxious, what makes you excited. Knowing this is the first step towards being able to make a change.

Then you can get to work on shifting your energy, and work towards feeling better.

Happiness and mental health

I remember going through periods of time in my teenage years where I felt hugely unhappy, and alone in that unhappiness. I now know that was a normal teenage experience, and possibly linked to hormonal changes going on in my body, and maybe also a bit to do with what was going on in my family circumstances at that time.

Mental health was not something we really spoke about at home.

Apart from one of my uncles who was a diagnosed scizophrenic.

I think my mum probably had a bit of depression when I was younger too, but it was never really discussed in the open, and I doubt she would be able or willing to discuss it now.

When I suffered with quite severe depression in my 30s, her attitude was:

"Pull yourself together and just get on with things."

Which wasn't helpful...or at least it didn't feel so at the time.

Again, not a dig...just an observation.

One of the worst thing about having depression and/or anxiety, is the frustrating yo-yoing between feeling like nobody cares and that you are completely alone, and feeling like a burden and someone to be pitied.

Yet depression is nothing to be ashamed of.

A quarter of the British population will experience some kind of mental health problem throughout the course of a year, with anxiety and depression being most common, according to the NHS Mental Health Network. Women are more likely than men to report ever having been diagnosed, and are most likely to access treatment and support.

There are, of course, lots of social factors why this is. However, as the Mental Health Foundation says, and which I also believe, women's readiness to talk about their feelings and their strong social networks can help protect their mental health. I wonder also, if a part of this is that women feel they *have* to carry on for the sake of others, so seek help sooner?

If you feel that you need support with your mental health, please don't be afraid to ask for help. At the back of this book you can find some UK-based resources and support groups.

Depression is a complex illness and doesn't just mean someone is unhappy. However, from my own experience, I know that working consciously on being happier, alongside keeping my health and wealth topped up, really helps me to keep my depression at bay.

I need constant daily reminders to keep my vibe high. Now, I am not for a minute suggesting that memes found on the internet or cute little post it notes with messages of "I love you" can ward off the black dog, but I do believe we should fill our minds with as many positive vibes as possible, in the hope that at least a few will stay there.

Here are a selection of my favourite quotes and affirmations that bring me joy and happiness.

"I like to read my diary occasionally to remind myself what a miserable, alienate old sod I used to be" **Jo Brand, Comedienne**

"Happiness can only exist in acceptance" **George Orwell**

"Folks are usually about as happy as they make their mind up to be" **Abraham Lincoln**

"Happiness is when what you think, what you say, and what you do is in harmony" **Mahatma Ghandi**

"They say a person needs just three things to be truly happy in this world, someone to love, something to do, and something to hope for" **Tom Bodett**

"Today was good, today was fun, tomorrow there is another one" **Dr Seuss**

Why not start your own file of happiness quotes, and get into the habit of using them as daily prompts?

Some final thoughts on wellbeing

Wellness is a pursuit. It is not a destination, rather a journey whereby the aim is to stay within a zone of relative ease, where health, wealth and happiness coexist and support one another, as the foundations to your life.

Too often wellness is marketed as a luxury, as something to aspire to....something illusive, only easily available to the rich and beautiful.

There are very few yoga videos that don't take place in a beautifully constructed set. Spa days in fancy hotels are pushed as the best way for women to unwind from the pressures of life. Even healthy eating options can use expensive ingredients such as chia seeds and wheatgrass.

It can mean that for many of us, wellness feels unaffordable and out of reach.

But there is no reason why it can't be ours too.

There are so many free and low cost options out there. It may take a bit of research and a bit more motivation to actually take action. Walking is free, as is doing yoga in your front room, or Tai Chi in the park.

We just have to decide that we want it, and find a way to make it a more routine part of our life….and where possible not wait until we are at breaking point to even start thinking about it.

Before I get you to commit to a new routine, a new programme, a new set of habits, I want us to take some time and look over what I like to call "my old shit".

Because I bet you are harbouring a whole heap of negative stories about wellbeing.

Stories about whether you are even deserving of health, wealth and happiness.

Plus, a bunch of stories from the people you have grown up around, shaping how you approach your own life.

Until you deal with some of that shit, you might find it quite tricky to move on.

The Power of Your Story

Do you ever just look at yourself in the mirror and be like
"How the fuck did I get here?"

Perhaps you have a clear picture of how you got to this point and are raring to go with a list of new habits to try.

Hold your horses.

We need to dig a little deeper still.

Ready to go again?

Take a deep breath, as we are about to head back in.

In this chapter we are going to unpack some of those "this is how that happened" and "well that's just the way I am" stories and see if these narratives are serving you, as you strive towards your BIGGER life.

We are talking here about not only understanding the life experiences that make you who you are, but also how the sharing of these where appropriate can help you fulfil you wider purpose in life.

I was a bit of a storyteller growing up.

Read into that what you like.

Some would say I had an active imagination, some would say as a child I was just an out and out liar. I like to believe I have a wonderful creative license over the events that go on in my life.

How often do you get to sit back and reflect on your life story? Or even get to share it with the world?

Not in an "I'm about to kick the bucket, so better get some things off my chest" kind of way.

Nor, in an "I'm a half-celebrity currently in the news, let me sell my soul for a few bucks" way either.

I am talking about giving yourself the time and space to really look at how you have got to this point and what it all means?

Would it surprise you to tell you I do it often?

For example, you may be thinking this is because I am a blogger, it's my job to be an open book and let people into my world.

Or you may think it is my work as a motivational speaker that enables me to unpack and repackage my stories for other people to use as inspiration or life lessons.

In my speaking, just like my writing, I have found the more I share of my personal story and life experiences, the bigger shifts my audiences experience, the more the message connects where it needs to.
You can probably think of lots of other people that you connect with because of their story?
Oprah Winfrey, Walt Disney, Steve Jobs, Tiger Woods, Richard Brandson... Yes, they were talented and have shared their many talents and gifts with us, but without us taking a peak into their worlds, perhaps we wouldn't buy into them so much.

The fact is though, I have always been this way. Long before I understood the power of storytelling as a tool for connecting with people.

I remember the time a school friend made fun of me calling out: "Jackanory, tell me a story" as I reminisced about something which we had experienced a few years prior. She said I was always at it: "Bringing up old shit."

What can I say, I like to make sense of the stuff I've been through.

I like to make connections, to link together the experiences and what I have learned from them. How they have shaped who I am, sometimes quite literally.

I realise I am quite strange in this desire though and have been told more than a few times "You read too much in to stuff" when I recall stories of childhood and share them with my siblings or close friends as a way of explaining something more current going on.

Somehow I find comfort in making sense of my life in this way, otherwise what is it all for?

I truly believe if more people on this planet had the time and inclination to think more deeply about the collective experience we called life, and were willing to take on board the various lessons that are gagging to be learned... Well, the world would be a much better place.

I know, call me a dreamer.

I am one.

And I encourage you to be one too.

Maybe by the end of this book you will become one.

For example, if I had to share with you the single most important thing I wanted growing up, it wasn't more cuddles, more toys, or even a better wardrobe, and trust me some of my hand-me-downs were shocking.

No, what I wanted most was to be heard. To really be heard. Which is ironic because I was quite possibly the loudest, most annoying, most outspoken of my siblings, much to the dismay of my parents who I am sure would have gagged me if given half a chance (I think my Dad did once with parcel tape to the amusement of everyone else).

Growing up in a large family is difficult when you want to feel important. Learning to share your attention between five other humans, whilst coping with the fact that one of your parents just up and left one day is pretty tough.

When I was just 11 years old, I proudly published my first-ever book, an autobiography called "One of Six", which I was tasked with writing as part of a school project in my first year of secondary school. I still have it now. It really wasn't very good, just a collection of mundane facts about my large east end family with a range of dodgy photos illustrating the first (and probably the most uneventful) decade of my life.

But I was in my element putting that masterpiece together. I could express myself however I wanted, I could open up my world to my English teacher who I could tell didn't quite get me, and best of all, they *had* to read it because teachers read all of our homework, right?

I would be heard.

Around eight years later, I found myself writing another autobiographical piece, this time to help secure a place at university – an opportunity that I didn't even know was available to me at first. I didn't think girls like me went off to get degrees.

I was a troubled 19-year-old with very little idea of what I wanted to do with my life. I wasn't particularly good at anything, with very few role models, and nobody really championing me.

This one particularly morning I found myself in Winchester along with 40 other potential entrants for the BA in Performing Arts. After completing some improvisation games, we were asked to submit a 3,000-word essay that the tutors would use to assess our passion for the arts and help them decide why they should have us on their three-year course.

We had two hours to write it, and could leave once it was submitted. I wrote a piece called "Everyday Drama" about the realities of living at home in my dysfunctional family in East London.

That writing did indeed secure me a spot on that course, and months later when I spoke to my new class mates about what their pieces had been about, I realised that while I had focused on me, they had submitted real academic pieces about the drama practitioners they admired or obscure pieces of poetry that had inspired their latest piece of classical music?

It just goes to show that sharing your unique take on the world can be incredibly powerful.

What would our world be without the brave souls who do this?

Who would be without the wonderful people who have come before us?

The wonderful women?

So what's your story?

Show me a woman who doesn't have a juicy backstory in this world. We all have one, even when we think we don't. And like it or not these stories shape us.

They shape how we behave, what we believe, and ultimately what we expect from the world, and everyone in it.

Check & Challenge 47 – What's your story

If someone asked you to sum up your life in just one paragraph what would it be? Write this in your journal. It could be in the style of an introduction to your autobiography or maybe even an obituary.

Over the past few years I have revealed more and more of my own story. It has helped me to connect with women around the world, but more than that it has helped me to make sense of myself.

I grew up believing that I was nothing more than a pain in the arse. I mean I was. I was a little cow. I was hard work. I was naughty, rude, and loved nothing better than pushing the boundaries.

I am now able to understand that within the context to which I was born, the external factors that were at play. It is easier I guess now to accept that part of me.

Being the mother of a five-year-old who has many of these traits, I often find myself asking the nature or nurture question, but at least I have the insight to know that many of the behaviours that tested the adults in my life when I was a child and teenager, eventually turned out to be the qualities that would go on to help me survive, and even thrive in the big bad world.

We do need to be mindful of where we let our stories take us though.

For a long period of my life, I had a "Poor Me" view of my back story. Now I don't see it that way so much.

I see what happened to me, or what I perceived as happening to me, as a blessing.

There are women with worst stories than mine. Stories of real hardship, abuse, neglect. But this is not a battle of the sad stories competition. Each of our stories has value. We don't have to have a difficult upbringing, a tragedy or a sad life to have a story that shapes us.

We don't need to be defined by our story.

We must learn to bravely and compassionately sit on top of our story, rather than have it stand on top of us.

For example, I think when you have been overweight for a while, or are just generally dissatisfied with how you look as a woman, you often have a range of revolving stories in your head...

- If I cared about myself I would eat better
- I don't know how to look after myself, I need help
- I am broken
- There is something wrong with me
- I am unlovable
- I should hide away

These are just stories, they don't have to be your reality.

Yes, we can blame the media and the diet companies, but a lot of the time these bullshit stories come from us, from inside our own heads.
Here are some of the bullshit stories I have told myself over the years:

- Fat people don't go backpacking
- Fat people don't do Triathlons/Tough Mudders/UltraMarathons
- Fat women can't become successful in business
- I can't be a fat motivational speaker
- I'm too large to wear a bikini
- My face is too fat for a short hair cut
- While I am at this weight I won't find a husband
- While I am at this weight I can't have a capsule wardrobe
- No point in getting my nails/hair/teeth done while I'm still fat
- I'm more likely to get a promotion or that contract if I was 14lbs lighter

I am not saying these statements are ever things I have said out loud, but they have most definitely featured in my inner chatter, preventing me from taking action, holding me back from the life that is out there and basically making me feel inadequate.

But at some point you just have to say "Fuck It" and give up those stupid excuses, disguised as stories, stories we use to self-sabotage.

Oh I have no self-control, so it is pointless me eating healthy as I will just ruin it next week
I'm not the kind of person who enjoys exercise
I can't stick to a plan
I don't like setting goals

Check and Challenge 48 – What is your predominant self-sabotaging story?

A great way of identify your predominant self-sabotaging story is to ask yourself questions always followed by another question, with the most important question of all being:

WHY?

Why are you fat/unhappy/unable to find a partner/messy (whatever it is you want to change)

And then you answer it with something like:

Because I eat too much
Because I hate the way I look
Because I'm ugly
Because I am lazy
Or whatever your own answer is (it doesn't have to be one of these)

And then you follow up that answer with the question of, but WHY?

It is the WHYing that helps you get to the CRYing in my opinion.

And crying is always a good thing. It is a release of emotion, and creates a shift.

I always feel better after a good cry. Don't you?

You might not get to your deepest, darkest self-limiting belief straight away. It might take some time. You might think it's one thing, but after more time doing this work you peel back the layers to find out it is something completely different.

In spring 2018, I went to San Diego to see world-renowned Transformational Coach, Lisa Nichols, at a conference. It was an incredible experience on so many levels. The conference was about establishing your personal brand as a speaker and writer, but it was also about unpacking some of the shit you carry with you.

One of the most powerful exercises we did was to find our most predominant self-limiting belief and then to counteract it.

Initially she asked us to scribble down what we thought it might be.

Mine was:

"I am not loveable".

Then she asked us to find evidence of that not being 100% true.

I thought about the love my daughter gives me, the love my siblings show, the small occasional displays of love from my mum, the love of my friends, and even the love that is out there for me in the work I do as a coach.

Nope.

The "I am not loveable" one was not going to cut it.

We then worked in pairs to talk through what else it could be, and bang like a blow to the stomach it came to me:

"I am not worth taking care of."

Now this comes from a range of things:

- My dad leaving when I was 11
- My mum being emotionally detached and not very hands-on in looking after me
- My ex-partner not supporting me or my daughter financially
- Friends who have left my life
- Employers who have let me down
- Feeling like nobody really cares about me
- Having to go through quite a lot by myself

And when I looked for evidence to the contrary, it was a lot harder to find. It was there, but I had to really search for it.

This realisation on its own was powerful enough, but what came next was out of this world.

We were then put into groups of four people, who Lisa called our "Earth Angels". Our chairs were positioned in such a way that one person would take the centre chair, and the others would sit either side and behind the person in the hot seat.

The person in the hot seat was asked to come up with a phrase that was the opposite of their self-limiting belief.

So mine would be:

"I am worthy of being taken care of."

Or

"I am worth taking care of."

Then this is where the magic started.

The person in the hot seat would state their phrase, and the other three would repeat it back to them like it was truth.

"Yes you are worth taking care of."

And this lasted for three whole minutes.

Now I am not going to lie, at first it felt a bit weird to have three strangers telling you something you only half believed to be true, but somewhere in the first 30 seconds I let down my guard and let those words sink in.

My dad should never have left, my mum should have been more emotionally available, my ex was wrong, is wrong for not supporting his child and leaving me to cope – all this was important. But the biggest breakthrough for me was that I should be taking better care of myself.

That was the game changer.

In life, people let you down, they don't behave as you would like them to.

However, ultimately we are responsible for our own happiness and we must prioritise that.

I am worthy of being taken care of, and if as an adult I can't do that for myself, how can anyone else?

Check & Challenge 49 – Change the soundtrack of your life

Self-limiting beliefs or sabotaging thoughts happen because we allow them to. We allow stories, some that are true and some that are not, to dictate how we feel about our lives.

We can change these stories.

We can change the record, so to speak.

It takes time and perseverance but it can be done.

Using positive affirmations daily is a great way to do this.

Listening to meditation recordings that send you gentle messages of love and empowerment.

Or creating your own recording of a mantra that you like.

Most of us have smart phones that give us the capability of recording audio. What you will need is a script of messages and somewhere quiet to record them. Record as much as you like but try to make it at least five minutes long, even if you are repeating yourself. If you want to be super snazzy you can add some relaxing background music, or the sound of nature.

Listen to this recording as often as possible.

For context, when I headed off to see Lisa Nichols, I had been doing work on myself for a number of years at this point. Working with therapist and coaches, leading and taking part in self-love programmes, and embracing the whole body positive movement.

These concepts were not completely new to me.

But the work is on-going.

Even the best coaches and leaders in the world need to constantly do this work. To revisit their self-limiting beliefs, and sabotaging stories.

I am not worthy
I don't deserve
I already have so much
Who am I to want more?

Whenever you reach for something new or embark on a new journey in your life, you will be confronted with fears and worries and so you will have to prepare yourself for some warfare. Stepping outside your comfort zone can bring unexpected issues, doubtful thoughts, uncertainty, and the feeling of never moving forward.

This is something we all need to recognize and see that every time we take it to another level, you have to expect there will be another level of discomfort.
Another level, another devil.

But the rewards are more than worth it.

That realization in San Diego that I am worth taking care of has changed everything. How I am looking after my mental and physical health, how I position myself in business, what I expect and look for in a future partner, and most importantly my relationship with my daughter.

A strange side effect of this work has been the ease that I have been able to forgive some of the people from my backstory, and accept that they were just doing the best they could with the resources they had to hand.

When you know better you do better right?

Blaming and shaming people into behaving better never works, it just helps you to hold onto resentment, fear and pain.

What if you can't let go?

I know that many of the women reading this book have had years of heartache over things which happened in their past. Relationship breakdowns, issues with parents, abuse. Feelings of not being good enough, not worthy of love, low self esteem.
Its OK for me to say let it go, but it's another thing doing it.
Working with a therapist or coach over a sustained period of time can be hugely beneficial, particularly if you have experienced severe trauma. Indeed, in cases like this, it can be essential. See the back of the book for resources that can help here.

Can you reframe any of your stories?

If I am being honest with myself, a few years ago I was letting my stories get the better of me. I was sensationalizing them, using them to serve my "poor me, poor me" narrative, as an excuse to stay down and not be my best self.
I realised that if I was to move on in my life, I had to change the narrative. I had to reframe my stories. The movie producer, Robert Evans, famously said:

There are three sides to every story: your side, my side, and the truth. And no one is lying. Memories shared serve each differently.

Check & Challenge 50 - which stories could you reframe?

Using the table below have a go at reframing some of the stories you like to tell so that they better serve your new BIGGER life.

What's the Story?	What does it tell me?	How could I reframe this?	

When I was around 12 years old and struggling with my parents divorce and the adjustment of going to secondary school, I started hanging around with a girl who was probably not the best influence on me.

Anyway, she got me involved in all kinds of scrapes.

One day on the way to school, we decided that we were going to bunk off and just hang out in a local park. Around midday we spotted a guy walking through the park with a box, we went over to see what was in the box and it was 10 tiny grey rabbits.
He was taking them to a local pet store to sell them. The pet shop was going to give him £0.50p each for them. We convinced him to sell two of them to us instead which he did.

Its funny, telling this story now it sounds so unbelievable.

Anyway, we played with these rabbits in the park all day and then at the end of the day we realised we would have to do something with them or our parents would know we had bunked off school.

But then we came up with a cunning plan.

We went back to my house and told my mum that on the way to school we had found the rabbits dumped in a public loo, and that we had rescued them.

My mum bought it hook, line and sinker, and even phoned the local paper who ran a story on it. We were hailed as local heros and even got pulled up on the stage in assembly at school.

I love telling that story...I have dined off it for years.

I come from a family of storytellers. My grandparents both told wonderful stories about the war. My nan's favourite one being about the man who was found in a bath tub in the street, naked and laughing, after a bomb had hit his home.

But the most notorious storyteller in my family was my great uncle Les, my nan's brother.

Now my nan on my mum's side came from a family of 18 children. I know right, 18. I can't imagine what it must be to carry, deliver and raise that many children.
My Uncle Les was child number 9.

180

Leslie Jerman was born in 1921. He was born to a father described as a poetry-quoting, library loving, gambler and womansier who delivered and sold newspapers at East Ham Station.

His mother (my great grandmother) had been in service as a girl, working as a maid.

Leslie read as many of his father's newspapers as possible and sold his first story at aged eight to the East Ham Advertiser for 10 shillings; and at age 16, he beat 199 other applicants to join The Scotsman newspaper as a copy boy.

He said, "Once I saw my name in print, I knew what I was going to do"

I felt very much the same after writing my first book, even if I didn't quite believe in myself enough to pursue a career as a writer back then.

He went on to become a renowned journalist reporting on a wide range of subjects, he contributed more that 12,000 entries in the Londoners Diary in the Evening Standard.

I only met my Uncle Les a handful of times. We became pen pals when I was about 10 after speaking briefly at a family wedding, where I asked him how I could become a writer like him. Nobody could have predicted the friendship that was formed that would last well into my 20s. Nor the impact his life and his stories would have on my own.

He supported me both financially and otherwise through university, becoming one of my greatest cheerleaders. He would send me photocopies of articles he had wrote, and often told me stories he had told me many time before, but it didn't matter. I can't tell you how nice it was to receive a letter from him typed on his faithful type writer, often with hand-amended scribbles with a fountain pen.

When he died in 2009, I was devastated.

At the funeral, his daughter Stacey, who I had never met in person, came over and hugged me tightly, telling me how special I was to him. She also told me not to grieve for too long as he had led a wonderful life.

I still miss him.

I wish I had insisted on spending more time with him.

I wish I had probed for more stories, especially stories about his early childhood

where it concerned my nan. I wish I had told him what an asset he had been. I wish he could see what I have achieved in the past 10 years.

I asked him repeatedly how I could become a writer, hoping he would give me a foot up, connect me to someone who could help me, but his advice was always the same,

"If you want to become a writer, Julie, you just have to write"

Annoying as that sounds it is true. Once I got over myself and just started writing regularly, my dream of becoming a writer came in to being.

He was a wise man.

When the elders in your family pass away you realise just what a resource they were,
and how much history and family stories die with them. It is such a shame that for so many people this awareness comes too late.

I believe that the stories from our forbearers are the key to our future.
Only when we can understand where we came from can be truly make an impact on our future.
Feeling that you are part of a story that is bigger than you is comforting, and helps us feel less alone.

So many cultures have a strong oral storytelling tradition, and I hope that with the rise in technology and our fast paced lives that these do not die out.

We must ensure they do not.

Check & Challenge 51 – Who are the storytellers in your family

Have a think about who tells the best stories in your family. Do you tell and retell
tales from your family history?

How can you preserve these stories?

Have a think specifically about the women in your families, what stories involve them?

You see I used to think the females in my family were all a little downtrodden, and had lives filled with struggle, and to some extent that is true. But if I look hard enough I can find stories of triumph, adventure and fearlessness.

That story of women being downtrodden was somehow serving me, because it gave me permission to believe my life had to be one of struggle too.

My story of struggle

Nothing quite prepares you for hitting rock bottom in your own life.

Even if it has been coming for a while you don't always appreciate its full magnitude until it is upon you by which time you are powerless to do anything remotely useful to pull yourself up.

That's how I felt just four years ago.

Long and painfully slow, like a rain drop making its way down a window pane, slowly my life had been falling apart.

No fan fair, no advanced warnings, nothing to see here, move along please... Luckily, my life imploded without too many other people noticing - or was it they just didn't care? Or were they just too busy dealing with their own shit?

Mid 2014, I slipped into a life I barely recognised, into an identity that sure as hell wasn't mine, into a world I didn't want to be in - and the worse thing of all - I let it happen, and I felt powerless to make any changes.

It all started when I lost my job, and not for the first time.

It was 2012, I was seven months pregnant and I was being made redundant from my well-paid public sector job, being made redundant for the fourth time in 10 years... OK, OK I get the picture...my services are no longer required!!!!

I got my first official job when I was 13. I worked in Forest Gate Wimpy for £1.50 cleaning dishes, serving customers and occasionally on a Saturday dressing up as Mr Wimpy and playing party games with children who were high on chocolate sundaes.

As difficult as I was as a child, you could never call me work shy.

I did all kinds of jobs to make sure I had money growing up. Checkout assistant in a supermarket, theatre usher, salad packer, barmaid... You name it, I have probably done it for a bit.

So you might think I would be a bit overwhelmed and perhaps a little embarrassed walking into Stratford Job Centre aged 36 to sign on. But I wasn't really, I just saw it as a bit of a new adventure. I figured a couple of months with some extra cash now my maternity pay had stopped would come in handy, and I assumed the advisors there would get me back into employment in no time.

Big mistake.

Sadly, they just didn't know what to do with me. I had close to a year ago been made redundant at seven months pregnant from a managerial position in a local authority working on the 2012 Olympics. When they looked at my colourful and varied CV showing 20 years of employment I almost wondered if they thought I was making it all up.

The first few weeks of signing on were a little annoying but bearable. Rose was still very small but there was no lift to get to the second floor where you had your interviews, so I had to carry her up, with all my bags etc. Trying to keep a toddler quiet and out of trouble while you are explaining for the fourth time that a retail job just wasn't going to work, became a little trying.

I played the game though, looking for proper employment the way I knew how to. I mean I hadn't been out of work EVER as an adult, something had always come along, and I often went from job to job with nice little promotions and pay rises along the way. I thought I was reasonably employable.

"Oh, but you haven't been using Job Search," the woman behind the Job Centre counter said to me one day.

"Erm no, I haven't. There are no jobs over £20,000 on Job Search," I said, followed by "plus the kinds of employment I am looking for just aren't listed there."

"Well Julie, your circumstances have changed now you might have to be more flexible" she said.

There was no way I was going to take a pay cut of more than 50% and move into an area of work I wasn't interested in, it just wasn't going to happen. So a battle of wills started to take place each fortnight, with myself and the advisor going round and round in circles.

It all came to a head one day when I went to sign on one day. It had been raining outside and I was a bit hot and flustered as Rose was playing up. When I asked at reception if I could go up to sign on, they said that my claim had been stopped and I would have to wait a certain amount of weeks to reapply (I can't remember the details now...I think I have blocked it all out).

At first, I was calm and asked if I could speak to an advisor about how it would affect my housing benefit and council tax relief, but they refused and said I could phone instead. Jobcentres don't pick up the phone...or maybe it was just me...maybe they just didn't pick up for me. I just wanted to know on what grounds they had cancelled my claim. I wanted to see that advisor and have her explain it to me to my face.

And in that moment I became THAT person.

If you have ever signed on or been in a government building around people trying to get their life back together, you will know THAT person.

It's the person that just loses their shit.

Now I am not normally an angry person, in fact I am quite reserved...don't like to make a fuss...but I was done with being treated like a nobody. Now I understood why the place had security, and why two out of the three phones on the wall had been ripped out of their sockets and were no longer in use.

"I am a person," I screamed.

"I am a real fucking person, can't you just treat me like an actual person?"

And that's when the three (yes three) security guards who I had seen for the last six months and nodded at, walked over to me and firmly escorted me out of the building.

My face was red, my eyes were brimmed with tears and my heart was pounding. I was so bloody angry.

I was angry at them, but also I was angry at me.

I had completely lost any sense of who I was. I had nothing to cling on to. No job. No social life. A relationship which was fast falling apart. I had never felt so alone in all of my life.

The following week I was asked to come back into the Job Centre as there had been a mistake and I would be allowed to sign on after all.

Part of me didn't even want to go back in that building.

But I had to.

In the week gone past I had found out that there was a scheme that you could be referred to from the Jobcentre if you were interested in starting up your own business. And I was interested in setting up my own business...boy was I ready to start up my own business.
I had been writing a blog for a number of years. I just had to work out a way to monetise it.

What followed was six months of filling in forms, creating a business plan, attending workshops which were so piss easy it was a joke, and then finally in June 2014, I received £2,500 start-up loan and Too Fat to Run was born.

I felt like I was a somebody again.

Look, this isn't your typical Rags to Riches story, but every day I walk past that building I am reminded of how close I was to losing everything and hitting rock bottom. I was literally weeks away from losing my home, the home I had worked for 10 years to achieve, I was so broke I was considering using the local food bank. Shit, I didn't even have a flipping pair of jeans that fitted me.

It is a million miles away from where I am today, just four years later, but I am reminded so often now that all you need is an idea and someone to believe in it, to help you out of the hole you can often find yourself in when life takes a nose dive like mine did.

I am also reminded that some people go through that shit week in week out, dealing with being spoken down to and not believed when they say they are looking for work. It is enough to break you, seriously it really is.

Today I am Julie Creffield, CEO & Founder of a global company, author of nine books, ultramarathon running, award-winning blogger. Oh, and transformational LIFE COACH!!!

I am a somebody. A somebody on a mission to change the bloody world.

I help ordinary women who are a little bit lost like I was to do extraordinary things with their lives. I help brilliant women work out what it is they really want and then give them the tools to do it. I help women live healthier, happier, wealthier, more adventurous lives. In the process of doing that, I make sure I never have to go in that bloody Job Centre or any other one like it ever again. That story is mine.

But equally it is not the only story.

When I first started writing my blog, it was the story of coming last in a race that inspired people. That single story was told a million times in newspaper and magazine articles, in blog posts, podcasts, TV & radio interviews.

I didn't even think it was that interesting as stories go.

But it captured the hearts and imaginations of women around the world who knew what it was to be the underdog, to fail, to want to do better.

I realised that if I was going to build a brand on next to no budget it would have to be via the power of storytelling.

And it has served me well.

When I leave this planet, I will be leaving behind a whole catalogue of stories for people to draw strength from, to learn from, and I am not done yet.

As a blogger and writer, I am now in a great position whereby pretty much anything could happen in my life, good or bad and it would eventually be turned into a positive and help others to grow.

You have that opportunity too.

Check & Challenge 52 – What stories of LIVING BIGGER do you want to be able to tell?

When we start to imagine the BIGGER, more EXCITING, more PURPOSE-FILLED life we want to lead, we get to create the stories almost before we play them out.

Write in your journal a story relating to your future self, almost as if someone was talking about you in years to come, what tales would you like them to tell?

But beware of those self limiting beliefs coming back, forcing you to play small, forcing you to minimize your dreams.

How can you start retelling the story from today?

You get to choose

I can remember when I met my daughter's dad and we first started discussing having children, during that glorious honeymoon period that most couples fall into, I can remember telling my now-ex about the kind of parent I wanted to be. The kind of life I wanted to lead.

Not one full of humdrum, domestic chores, routine, but one where we didn't follow the rules, where we parented in the way we wanted to, taking our child on adventures, teaching them things about the world that no school could teach, making time for each other and our separate goals and aspirations.

I was able to see it so clearly in my minds eye.

My ex... not so much.

Even though he is a talented writer, singer, and actor, and someone with a relatively free and creative spirt. He just couldn't see this vision I had for our future together.

Maybe it was because he had children from previous relationships and wasn't as naïve as I was about the strain having children has on a relationship, how much you have to compromise, how logistically so many of your dreams become difficult to implement once you have little people in your life.

However, I stand by those dreams.

A few years later, when I did indeed find myself pregnant, and by then unemployed, I no longer dreamed these dreams, because I was now consumed with worry and fear about simply being able to keep my head above water.

Reality had set in BIG TIME.

I now had all these stories about who I would become once my child came along, all these things that I would no longer be able to do...

- I wouldn't be able to travel
- I wouldn't be able to do things without the baby in tow
- I would never have money for me
- I wouldn't be able to treat myself or prioritise my needs
- I wouldn't be able to further my career or build a business
- I wouldn't be able to have fun or adventure
- I wouldn't be able to achieve goals

I realise now that these were 100% just stories.

For sure, some of these things have been harder than others, but I have not let becoming a parent and even a single parent stop me from living the life I want to live.

Of course I do need to compromise, I do need to put other peoples needs and desires alongside mine, but I realised I was using those stories as a way of staying in my comfort zone, doing what was expected of me, using them to bolster my "Poor me, Poor me" single parent status.

Check and Challenge 53 – What are the things you tell yourself you can't have?

Make a list of as many things you tell yourself that you can't have in life. Don't make any judgements, don't try and convince yourself otherwise. Just list as many as you can think of.

We will revisit these in Chapter 8.

Sharing your story

Not everyone has a story they are willing to share with the world on the kind of scale that I have. But this doesn't mean you can't use your experiences to help you grow and develop, and to add value to your life and the lives of those around you.

One of the reasons I began blogging back in 2010 was because I felt I had a story to tell that wasn't really been told, I never could have imagine to what extend people would connect with that story, connect with me.

It started off as being quite a selfish pursuit, to motivate me to run more, to keep me accountable on my weight loss journey. But it soon became much more about other women, and that's when it really started to grow in popularity.

In recent years, I have used the online platform I built to tell the stories of other women too, because their stories are equally as powerful as mine, even if they themselves don't always believe that to be true.

Such as the story I told about Nikki who ran the London Marathon in 2018 and was fat shamed mid-way through. She finished the race in darkness, it taking her 11 hours to complete. Her story was seen by more than a million people, and enabled an incredible conversation about plus-size fitness and resilience.

Telling your story to an audience of people who care, and maybe some that don't, has to be the most powerful medicine on earth. As humans, by default we are a constantly unfolding narrative, a hero in a story that no one else can write.

And yet so many of us leave our stories untold, we keep our experiences to ourselves because we are scared of being judged for them, or we worry that nobody else will even care, or that they would care too much.

The same is true when we don't speak up about our thoughts and opinions. I believe that when we keep our stuff to ourselves, we wind up feeling lonely, isolated, out of touch with our purpose, out of alignment. It may even contribute to feelings of being unworthy, unloved, or broken.

Sharing your story is cathartic. It enables you to show up authentically, and does wonders for your self-esteem.

When people feed back that your story touched them, or that they have had something similar happen to them, it helps you remember that **you are not alone - even if sometimes you believe you are.**

Check & Challenge 54 – How could you tell your story?

There are lots of ways of recording your story, and sharing it (or not)

- Blogging
- Short story
- Memoir
- Interviewed
- Speaking
- Talking to family members
- Scrapbook
- Art
- Song writing
- Microblogging/social media
- Contributing to archives and museums

Which of these would you consider?

I have built an incredible life through the power of telling my story.

It has taken time and courage to get to the point where I can show up 100% as me, but boy has it been worth it.

Whether we like it or not, we will go through this life adding to the narrative of this world. The big question is: how do we want it to play out?

Remember that scene with Cameron Diaz in the film The Holiday where she plays out her life through the medium of film trailers? I often use this as a useful reminder that we get to construct so much of the way our story pans out.

How would the trailer for the story of your life look and sound?

And if you don't like how it is currently shaping up - what ya gonna do about it?

Curating a Life Full of Adventure

I might not know what I want, but I sure as hell know what I don't want

When I was a child one of my favourite things to do was to get lost.

No, seriously, I mean it.

My mum told me a story of when I was five-years-old and I hid under a clothing rail for an hour in a department store, while she and the staff run around like crazy trying to find me.

A few years later I cycled my bike almost three miles from Upton Park to Barking, where I proceeded to join the dual carriageway, ended up on a flyover, and had to be escorted off by police and returned home.

I was always trying to disappear, always trying to run away.

Not because I hated home, or my family, but because I wanted adventure. I wanted excitement.

Of course I didn't really understand that back then, but now it's clear as day. It didn't help that I was an avid reader and had a very active imagination. I once got a set of children's Encyclopedias for Christmas, something my siblings laughed at but that I thought was the greatest gift imaginable. I also loved the author, Enid Blyton who wrote the Famous Five novels and the Wishing Chair series, fuelling my need for excitement and the unknown.

If I had known that being an adventurer was an actual thing, then I would have 100% gone for that as a career. As it stands, I climbed both a glacier and a mountain this year; so I reckon I just took the scenic route to find my ideal job.

Welcome to Chapter 8.

I have been referring to this chapter throughout the whole book because it is somewhat of a key chapter.

Some people are born into lives full of adventure and excitement; others have to curate them for themselves, defining what it is to feel alive, to feel like there is still much to explore, to discover.

So strap yourself in.

It's time for you to really start thinking big, to start getting excited about what the future might hold, and ultimately to ask yourself if you are really willing to be bold and do something amazing with your life.

This is about starting to curate the life you have always imagined for yourself. It doesn't require climbing a mountain, running a marathon, or travelling to the other side of the globe. It can be about smaller but equally as important things, such as treating yourself to that dress you've always wanted, forging new friendships or committing to going for a walk every morning before work.

Either way.

Buckle up. It might get a bit bumpy around here.

Knowing what you want

Last year I delivered an afternoon's workshop to an audience of 80 school business managers in the Midlands. I give talks and run workshops to all sorts of groups, but when I landed this gig I got a bit exciting because this was a profession I knew a little bit about, as both my mum and my sister work in school administration.

I gave a talk in the morning to the whole group all about Thinking BIG and overcoming adversity, and then in the afternoon I led a break-out group on Setting and Achieving Big Fat Stupid Goals.

It was brilliant, even if I do say so myself.

These were my women. I could feel it, and they could feel it. These were middle-aged women (of all shapes and sizes) from different school settings across a large geographical area. They didn't know each other, so there was a risk they wouldn't feel comfortable enough to share in this type of environment, but for some reason they did.

After a few minutes warming them up, I started off with some light touch interaction in pairs to talk about their biggest barriers to health and happiness. Then once they were warmed up, I served them a bit of a curve ball with the question:

"If I could give you anything to make you happy, what would you like?"

I told them they mustn't think about how, they just had to imagine I was their fairy god mother and that whatever they wished for they could get. And this is where the fun bit started.

I asked them to start sharing their answers, and we had everything from:

"I'd like to buy a mobile home and travel around Europe".

To...

"I'd like a Mulberry handbag".

To...

"I'd like my headteacher to bugger off and retire", which of course got a great amount of laughs and cheers.

The thing with this activity is that it energises a group.

OK, they might start off a bit apprehensive feeling like they might be judged for wanting stuff for themselves, but once they get over that they can't stop themselves. You end up with women nodding along with each other's desires and they start writing down all these wonderful ideas.

I closed the session with some simple instructions for how to turn these goals into real life, how to use my Big Fat Stupid Goals principles to actually make them happen, and we all left that workshop on a high.

Just as I was packing away my things a lady came over to me to ask a question. She was fighting tears. I pulled her to the side of the room and asked if she was OK, she replied:

"Yes, I am fine. I just wanted to say thank you".

I enquired as to what had made her so upset and she replied,

"I don't think anyone has asked me what I actually want in over 20 years"

And then it was me holding back tears.

She explained how she had literally forgotten that she could want stuff too, and that she didn't need to focus all of her energies and attention on her children, husband and parents, that is was OK for her to want things to enhance her life too.

Wow, Wow, Wow, Wow, Wow.

I will never forget that woman. I will never forget the power of just posing the question.

What do you want?

What do you really want?

Check & Challenge 55 – Tell me what you want, what you really really want

So come on then, tell me, in the simplest of forms. What do you want? What is the thing that you most desire in your lifetime?

How easy was that to decide on?

Did it come to you straight away?

Or was it a bit of a struggle?

Knowing what you want from life should be the simplest thing, right? Yet for so many of us it can be a real challenge to actually pin down the things we really yearn for. Often we know what we *don't* want, but being able to verbalise what we *do* want is seemingly impossible.

Why is that?

Like knowing what you want for Christmas each year as an example.

One of our favourite pastimes as children growing up was flicking through the Argos catalogue and sharing with each other what we wanted.

We would start off in the garden furniture section, following the unspoken rules of the "Argos Catalogue Game" which were, you only get to choose one item, you can't choose something someone else has chosen, and you have to be able to explain why you would want it.

We'd make our way through the jewelry, the household goods, and the furniture, before eventually getting to the really good bits, the toys and board games.

That activity kept us occupied for hours.

The thing is it didn't really matter if there was any chance of us ever acquiring any of these items. It was just fun to dream, to visualise a time when perhaps we could just pick and choose the things we desired.

So how come we can't do that now?

Have we been taught somewhere along the line that to want things is greedy? That we should be grateful for what we have? That we will only become disappointed or annoyed if we can't get the things we want?

How many times have I heard women tell me they didn't really ask for anything from their partner at Christmas time, or they have given up on wanting a certain type of experience, because the kids have to come first, and there is always something else to spend money on.

I believe that one of the simplest ways of Living a Bigger Life as a woman is to take on an attitude of adventure.

To be adventurous in your thinking, your actions and in your relationships. Stretching and growing into the very best version of you, wherever the opportunity arises.

I have worked with more than 10,000 women through the various online and in person programmes I run, and when it comes to my coaching, the women who come to me tend to fall into one of three groups,

1. Women who already have BIG goals in mind but have never had the confidence, courage, or commitment to pursue them
2. Women who can easily come up with a goal once given some time and space to consider it, and who need support to help map out how to achieve them
3. Women who literally have no idea what they want from life or how to get it

Like seriously.

The women in this third group are clueless when it comes to setting themselves a goal. They have no big travel desires, no urge to change career, are not driven by a big material purchase, or to set up a side business, or learn a new skill.

They want to have goal, but they tell me they are just not goal-orientated, and often tell me they want something much less tangible with phrases such as:

"I just want to be happy." or "I just want to be healthier." or "I just want to feel better about myself."

Now I am not going to lie, I find it much more challenging working with these ladies, because my default way of thinking is very goals-orientated. Plus, as much as women have told me I have special powers, I can not wave a magic wand and get these things for them.

If I want to feel happier, I plan something BIG which I know will make me happy (even if it is only in that moment). If I want to improve my health I set myself a BIG fitness goal whereby I know improved health is a side effect. It is just how my brain works.

What about you?

How are you wired when it comes to setting yourself goals?

The power of saying yes

Are you a yes person or a no person?

Are you a positive Polly, or a negative Nellie?

For a long long time I was a bit of a NO person and a Negative Nelly

When friends suggested things to do, or opportunities arose through work, my initial reaction was quite often all the reasons why I couldn't or shouldn't do something. My default was often to think about the worst case scenario or to convince myself that it would all end in tears, so probably best to stick to what I know.
So I said NO or I found an excuse to not partake.

Paint balling, horse riding, learning a new skill, a weekend away - they all sound great in principle but what if they don't turn out how I expect? Plus, isn't this all a bit self-indulgent? Shouldn't I be working hard, thinking sensibly and saving for a rainy day?

I always thought I had time.

Like, I would do these fun things once my life really got going.

After school, after college, after uni, when I got my next job, when I met my future husband, when I moved into my new home – and, of course, when I lost my weight.

Notice I said "my" like it's mine and you can't have it?

198

I think this all came from a deep-seeded belief that I didn't really deserve nice things, or that amazing experiences didn't happen to people like me.

There were also further blockages about being able to afford to pay for such treats. I would assume things were more expensive than they actually were, or worry that if I spent a large sum of money on something like a holiday, knowing my luck a week later a massive unexpected bill would come through the door.

You could say in my early 20s, I very much had a lack mentality.

I wanted a more exciting life filled with adventure and excitement, but I was too scared to actually change some of my beliefs and just make it happen. I was scared of failure, but I was also too comfortable in my "waiting to be saved" mindset, with my stories of being hard done by.

This changed in the most bizarre way one evening when I was in my late 20s.

I had organised a house party to celebrate my birthday, and around 20 or so of my friends came over to my place for drinks and food, including a girl called Natalie who I had spent a bit of time with back in my clubbing days. I didn't know her very well at all as she was more of a drinking pal than a friend I spent any real time with.

In the early hours of the morning when we were all under the influence and talking rubbish, she told me she was going to visit her half-brother in Colombia in a few weeks time. Me in my drunken state, said:

"I want to come." .

A few days later she called me and said:

"Were you serious about coming to Colombia with me? I'd love for you to come with me."
And despite not knowing her or her brother very well at all, and having enormous fears about travelling to South America I responded:

YES

I don't know what came over me.

A month later I jumped on a plane and I spent three amazing weeks in Cali having all kinds of adventures, and I also made a real friend for life, all through the power of YES.

That was a huge turning point for me, and I become much better at seeing opportunities for what they are, instead of filling my head with all the negative stories such as: "I can't afford it", "But what about work", "I won't know anybody there."

I booked a holiday alone to St Lucia one Christmas because I didn't face spending it alone in the UK; I decided to start renting out my spare room; I set up a business as a consultant; I started going to night school to learn Spanish, I took myself off travelling around South East
Asia despite having not lost the weight I thought I needed to.

I just decided I had held myself back for too long.

One of the ladies from my Living a Bigger Life Mastermind Group has a similar list.

"By saying YES, I have: travelled the world; landed myself a dream job in TV; set up my own business; interviewed Sinitta live on stage in front of 1,500 women; swum with dolphins in the ocean; partied in a fancy apartment with a rooftop swimming pool; interviewed our Prime Minister at No 10 Downing Street; written a successful business book; and moved to a beautiful riverside home in southwest France that has its own island.

"And that's not even the exhaustive list. I'm not mega wealthy – far from it – so this hasn't been about having loads of disposable income. Also, I'm not totally fearless. Some of the things I've said yes to have required a very deep breath before I jumped in, but the feeling you get when doing something that is both scary and exciting, knowing that you are really living and making the most of this wonderful life we've been given, it's exhilarating."

Check & Challenge 56 – Where is on your travel list?

Many people dream of travelling to far-flung places around the world, but not everyone realises these goals. The first step to getting somewhere is knowing where you want to go. List 10 places you would love to travel to in the next year. They don't have to be overseas– your home turf could be just as ripe for exploring.

Remember this is not an opportunity for you to be realistic or negative about the possibility of these happening - we are just dreaming at this stage. You can use this list for an exciting activity we are going to do later in this chapter.

My top 10 places I would like to travel to are:

- Aruba

- Tokyo
- Kenya
- Shetland Islands
- Colorado
- Norway
- India
- Bali
- New Orleans
- Canada

Now this might be a good place for me to talk about bucket lists. I am not a great fan of them, because a bucket list is simply a list of things you want to do before you die which I think:

1. Is quite morbid
2. Implies you have ages to tick them off (unless you are about to die)
3. Creates an attitude of wishful thinking rather than action

I prefer to use a simple technique of setting manifestation lists every 12 weeks.

In theory, they work like a bucket list in that you write down what you want and outline your manifestation goals. However, then you have to:

1. Believe 100% that it is going to come to you
2. Be open to something better than what you asked for instead
3. Take inspired action
4. Be as visible as you can with your goals

The first manifestation list I ever wrote down looked like this.

1. A new man who is right for me
2. A sponsor for Runner of the Month (one of my initiatives)
3. A holiday with Rose *
4. A cleaner I can trust *
5. A business manager *
6. A fully paid speaking gig *
7. A Range Rover Evoke
8. The house of my dreams
9. A personal trainer *
10. Some new friends *
11. £50K in the bank
12. A fully paid trip to the States *

Now the *asterisk represents the items on this list that I managed to attract into my life. Some of them took a little longer than 12 weeks, but I still think seven out of 12 is pretty good going.

And when I look at the ones I didn't achieve, in part I think I wasn't clear on how much I really wanted those things anyway; some of them were things I thought I should want, and for many I wasn't really up for putting in any work to achieving them.

Because that is the thing - you can't just leave it up to the universe, you have to play your part too.

For example, in Chapter 4 I talked about a book I read called *The Celestine Prophecy*, which I absolutely manifested into my life.

Here is the string of events which led to it becoming mine:

- Bloke I met by chance recommended it
- He lent me his copy
- I read half of it before giving it back
- Amazon had just started something called a wish list, I added that along with four other books I wanted
- I never managed to find it in an actual book store
- Christmas came round and I opened a present from one of my aunties, and it was the book
- She didn't understand why I was so surprised by it
- My mum had sent her the Amazon list.
- It was the only one from the list my aunt could find in a book store

You see the world works in mysterious ways.

If you believe in God, or the universe, or some people call it source, you know that they will be conspiring to bring you everything you want as long as you are clear on what exactly it is you want, and are willing to meet them half way.

Other things I've manifested over the last few years by simply having them on my list:

- The perfect first date
- A great babysitter for Rose
- A session with a stylist
- A new sofa
- The perfect pair of going out shoes

202

- An Apple watch
- A new website
- A spot delivering the closing keynote at a conference I wanted to speak at

Now the skeptic in you might just say well its luck, or I simply got out my credit card, but I truly believe the moment you get clear on what you want - like crystal clear - sometimes it simply falls into your lap.

Check & Challenge 57 – Create your very first 12 in 12 manifest list

Sit and write a list of 12 things you want. Don't think about how, just focus on the feeling you will have when you have these things in your life. Make sure you make a note of the date in 12 weeks time where you can review your progress.

Look at the list as often as you can, and imagine your life with these things in it. Also keep your eyes out for clues, the universe will test us to see if we actually want the things we say we do.

Surely it's not as simple as that?

I have a resounding belief that opportunities come to me at the exact right time they need to, and that they have come about to teach me something about myself or the world that we live in that I really need to learn. This means I am much more relaxed about international travel, meeting new people and having new experiences than I used to be.

Fear of the unknown holds so many of us back. Fear of judgment from others about the choices we make can also be a big problem, especially for women, and especially for mothers who have to juggle being the caregiver to their child and fulfilling their own wants and needs.

A few years back, one of the things I put down on my manifest list was:

"An all-expenses press trip, somewhere I have never been before."

Please note this was before I had done any overseas trips for work.

Literally four days after writing this down, an email enquiry came for me to spend five days in Israel on a press trip to review the Jerusalem Half Marathon. I had never been to the middle east, I would have to organise childcare, I was to be the only journalist from the UK out of a group of 40 from around the world, and the race had some massive hills on the course - all things which might put me off.

But do you know what? Life is too short to be turning down potentially life-changing opportunities.

Do I ever say no?

There is absolutely a place in my life for big fats NO's. I quite easily turn opportunities away which don't feel right for me. A few months ago, for example, I turned down a trip to Switzerland to take part in a three-day race across the mountains. This wasn't a good fit, it was a busy time for me at work and my fitness wasn't where I needed it to be. I didn't fancy being air-lifted off the mountain via helicopter due to a twisted ankle. It was just too much of a risk in this case.

It is just as important to know what you do not want. However, always try to frame this from a position of what you want, rather than what you don't want.

For example, it's like when you are dating. If you were looking for a new romantic partner for example you would ask for:

- Tall
- Dark
- Handsome
- Generous
- Adventurous

Rather than

- Mustn't be short
- Don't like blondes
- Hope he's not ugly
- Can't be unemployed
- Can't be a bum

The universe doesn't really understand negative thoughts/phrases like this. In some ways because you are focusing on those things, it sends you more of that. So be careful where you focus your attention.

I believe our focus on, "I don't want to be FAT" is exactly the same.

Words I focus on for better health and a body I love are:

- Strong
- Lighter

- Healthier
- Nourished
- Confident
- Beautiful

Be open to good stuff coming in to your life.

Have faith that good things are meant for you and will work out fine (better than fine).

Buddha is often quoted as saying:

"What you think you become
What you feel you attract
What you imagine you create"

When I first set up my blog back in 2010 I had no idea my life would pan out the way it did. A few years later when I had the huge task of turning my blog into a viable business, I knew I had to back myself, I knew I had to create some hype, I knew I had to stand out from the crowd.

I was once in a training course for running coaches, and at the end of the session we were asked to share a goal we had, in terms of using this new run leader qualification, I said:

"I want to become the world's leading expert on plus-size running"

The other people in that room laughed, but I was dead serious.

Often as women, our problem is we find it hard to imagine a life different from the one we live, different from the lives of the people around you. If I had grown up knowing adventurers, people who skied, people who ran marathons, perhaps I would have thought this possible for me sooner.

I can't think of a single woman during my childhood who ran her own business.

Sometimes we have to find our inspiration further afield. The fact we have the internet and media resources that we do, means we no longer have this as an excuse.

Check & Challenge 58 – Who would you be, if you weren't you?

Make a list of five to 10 women you admire, who are leading exciting lives similar to the ones you would like for yourself. These do not have to be famous people or celebrities, they can just be women you know.

My role models for some time have been (and if you don't know who these people are, look them up and follow them on Instagram)

- JK Rowling
- Beyonce Knowles
- Adele
- Denise Duffield Thomas
- Katie Price
- Lily Allen
- Jessamyn Stanley
- Karren Brady
- Julie Holmes
- Bryony Thomas

Now the thing is, your role models don't have to be people other like or admire. Half the UK hates ex-glamour model Katie Price, and I am not 100% behind every decision she has ever made in her life. However, I admire her business sense, and the fact she doesn't give a shit what others think about her.

The final two ladies on this list are likely to be women you do not know, these are women who are friends of mine. They started of as acquaintances, and then colleagues, and then we became friends and they continue to inspire, motivate and drive me to be the best version of myself.

The fact I am around them in person, seeing them grow awesome businesses is incredibly powerful, and equally I know my work inspires them too.

Check & Challenge 59 – Channel your best you

Think about the woman you want to become, and put yourself in her shoes now. Channel how it must feel to be her, and use her as your guide for making decisions, feeling confidence, and taking action.

When I did this exercise with some women on my retreat a few years ago, one of my ladies said, I already do this; I channel Beyonce. If I get into a situation where I am nervous, or feeling a bit inadequate, I think to myself "What would Beyonce do?"

So if you find it hard to picture your future you borrow the persona of someone from your list above for the time being.

A word about other people and your dreams

We are really naive if we think we can go through life on our own, making decisions that only affect us. Very few women ever get to do this. We often have to be considerate of others, and put their needs before ours.

But we should be able to have some level of autonomy over the direction of our lives, even if it does affect our loved ones, especially as they often get to reap the rewards of our successes too.

When we put our head above the parapet, and look to make changes in our lives, often it is the views of others that we consider first.

What will people think?
What if people won't like this new me.
What if my success makes people feel like I am a bitch or not like them?
What if my goals and dreams make me come across as selfish?

Someone once told me that what other people think of you is none of your damn business. However, often we really do want to know what others think of us, we want to understand how we are seen by the world through the eyes of others, and - most importantly - if we are being judged fairly or otherwise.

As humans, of course, we are being judged by ALL of us, but the sooner we get over ourselves, stop caring so much about what others think of us and get on with living our lives, the better for everyone.

We know that women let their fears of being judged stop them from living the lives they truly want. To avoid being judged we often try to blend in, we try to please, we try to shrink to fit a mold that is simply impossible to fit in to, and in the process we become invisible and forget who we are.

Remember people don't always want you to succeed

Even the people closest to you. In fact, especially the people closest to you sometimes.

How often has someone you loved played down your accomplishments, or ignored them all together? How often has a friend or colleague told you not to think too big in case you get disappointed?

This is often not about you, but about them and how they view themselves. By you being great, you are literally holding up a mirror to them to see the things they wish they could do with their lives but are to afraid to do.

Or perhaps they have fears about you changing and leaving them behind.

Mark Twain said:

"Small people try to belittle your achievements, but great people make you believe in your greatness. Surround yourself with those people, even if they can't see what you see, they see you."

You can not go through life worrying about other people.

Not everyone will fall in line with your vision - even if you really want them to.

Be patient. Get on with just doing you. It can take time for others to see you and your potential. Oh, and one more important thing.

Don't be afraid to piss people off.

The only way to avoid pissing people off is to do nothing, and chances are many people still won't be happy then either.

I have found that my biggest adventure so far in life has been in negotiating the difficult path that are relationships. For me the Living a Bigger Life concept, especially the Living a Bigger Life Quadrant tool, has helped me to

- Form stronger bonds
- Get rid of people who are no good for me
- Seek out exciting new friends
- Be kinder
- Be more authentic
- Be more open

Some of the most challenging decisions I have had to make over the last few years have been born from a desire to live a bigger more authentic existence, and that has often hurt or pushed people away from me. In some instances I have simply grown away from people and of course that can be hard at first.

But as the saying goes:

"People come into your life for a reason, a season or a lifetime."

Only we get to decide which is which.

Sometimes we have to clear out the old to make room for the new. Sometimes we have to get clear on the kind of people we want in our life, the people we need to help us grow, because otherwise life becomes stagnant.

Check and Challenge 60 – Build a network of dreamers and believers

Who do you know in your life that has big dreams too? Who are the positive people? The builder uppers, not the tearer downers? Who can be a sounding board? Who can contribute to your ideas, or simply listen to them without judgement?

Stick to these people like glue.

Make excuses to be with them as often as possible.

And if you don't have any women like this in your life right now, go find some.

Places to find them:

- Online forums
- Networking events
- Meet-ups
- Singles holidays (not the ones for hooking up, the ones for people travelling alone)

It is quite possible that some of the existing women in your life could be just as supportive, if given the tools and if supported to achieve their goals too.

Check & Challenge 61 – Host a Living Bigger Life "Big Night In"

What is a big night in? And surely I should be encouraging you to go out right?

So here's the thing.

When was the last time you had a whole evening with no kids, no partners, no whinge bags, no bitches?

When was the last time you spent time with women that you love, admire, and are intrigued by, and spoke about stuff that really mattered?

When were you able to do that without having to compete with loud music, or waiting staff, or some kind of activity which took centre stage?

In this busy life we lead, our female friendships often take a back seat. Our dear friends sometimes move away, get busy with their own life. We drift apart... and it's hard to make new friends, right?

Yes, we organise social gatherings, but they are often to celebrate birthdays or other occasions. You don't always get an opportunity to just sit and be with each other and to give and receive the emotional support we so often crave.

Big Nights In encourage 12 key qualities of friendship AND give you the opportunity to share with each other your dreams and aspirations for the future, free from judgement.

Big Nights in enable you to:

- **Be you.** The greatest gift you can give to others and to yourself is to be you —the REAL you.
- **Be understood.** You can help your friends understand you better, and in turn get to understand them better too.
- **Be accepting**. This is a great opportunity to celebrate what makes you different, the perfect opportunity to invite friends from different backgrounds, faiths, social situations.
- **Be available.** Our busy lives make time a very precious commodity. These regular meetings help you switch off your phones, switch of external influences and be truly present for each other.
- **Be giving**. What can you do for another that will make their life better? How can you give practical help? What doors can you open for them? And be open to them doing the same.
- **Be interesting.** Between meetings you will work on yourself, take action and be brave, so you have something to share with others
- **Be a listener.** You will learn the skills needed to really listen to your friend. Not spending their talking time thinking about what you're going to say next that is about you.
- **Be positive.** People like to be around people who makes them feel better, not someone who poisons their time together with toxic negativity. Positivity is infectious.
- **Be honest**. When a friend's actions or decisions scare you, you will be able to share your heart in a non-judgmental way. If not you, then who?
- **Be appreciative**. Tell your friends how much they mean to you. You may think they already know this, but a verbal affirmation every so often makes sure they do.
- **Be respectful**. You and your friends may not have the same likes and dislikes in people, politics, or passions. Be respectful of these differences.

- **Be supportive**. Cheer friends on when they "win," cry with them when they "lose," and laugh with them when either of you do something stupid.

I could write a whole book on the power of this one key concept, but instead I have created a resource pack you can access on the website, **www.juliecreffield.com/LBLresources** to help you do this properly.

Let's build up a back catalogue of learning from these gatherings and share them on social media using the #iblamejulie, #livingabiggerlife and #bignightin hashtags. I would love to see these in action.

But while you are here and reading this book, let's look at one of the fundamental objectives from the Living a Bigger Life way of life, a tool which can be applied time and time again, which is perfect for sharing in the big night in format - that of setting and achieving your Big Fat Stupid Goals.

But what exactly are they?

And how are they different from normal goals.

Big Fat Stupid Goals

I have always been a planner, and a bit of a goal setter but growing up I would often hear conflicting messages about how best to achieve your dream.

There was the the incremental way of doing things: the slowly-slowly, catchy-monkey approach to life. You know, making small but consistent steps everyday until eventually you reach your goal

Or

There is the aim for the moon approach. If you miss the star, you'll still go further than if you didn't aim so high. THINK BIG...off the scale BIG. The one that is more about exponential growth.

So which one is best?

Well, I guess there is value in both of them, because "We are what we repeatedly do" after all, but I seriously think there is some value in choosing goals that absolutely scare the living daylights out of you once in a while.

But why?

Big Fat Stupid Goals are goals that are BIG in scale, FAT as in the luxurious good-for-you type, and STUPID because folk will be shaking their heads in disbelief at the sheer thought of you doing it.

They make you feel sick with excitement. The moment they pop into your head, you know things are about to change. You know that quite possible nothing will be the same again, they will change you in some way, in the best of ways.

The point is to think BIG, but to break things down into a range of equally ambitious tasks, in what I like to call My Massive Milestones.

Check & Challenge 62 – Do you already have a BFSG?

Its quite possible that you already have a goal suitable to become your BIG FAT STUPID GOAL. But if you have, how come you haven't achieved it?

Ask yourself

- Why?
- What's stopping you?
- What has to happen first?
- How long will you wait?

Often we have things we desperately want to do and achieve in life, but we let our lack mindset get in the way of acting upon them:

I don't have enough money
I don't have enough time
I don't have enough skill
I don't have enough support

But there is always enough when you open yourself up to finding what you need from unexpected sources. When you open up to receiving (this is often our problem as women we are so used to giving we have forgotten what it is to take).

Somehow we feel like letting other people help is failing, like we have to do everything ourselves. Even though we know the wonderful gift of being in service and helping others our self.

I bet there have been times in your life where you have been offered things you have wanted but you have said no because it hasn't come in the format that you expected, or you felt like you were not ready, that you somehow didn't deserve it.

Practice saying YES to some small stuff to get you into practice, say YES to the colleague who invites you out for lunch. Say YES to the man who offers you his seat on the tube. Say YES to the distant friends who has a spare ticket for a gig tonight.

This is what it is to receive.

Go back to those stories from Chapter 7.

There is one woman in my Living a Bigger Life Mastermind who felt extremely uncomfortable receiving presents on her 40th birthday. It was her birthday, a big birthday at that, for goodness sake, and yet she told me that accepting gifts from her friends and family made her feel like she owed them something.

This seems quite common, as another 40th birthday party I went to the instructions were to bring non-perishable food items to donate to the local food bank, a brilliant cause no doubt, but I am sure many of her friends and family would have also liked to have showered her with gifts.

Accepting help when it is offered

My story of always having to do everything myself, not having anyone to support me, to carry the load, is simply a bullshit story, but it is one that I work hard at maintaining at times.

I remember one time I was travelling on the tube somewhere with a heavy suitcase, and I also had a strained back. A man offered to help me with it, and I almost said "No, I'm fine" and I thought, "Actually I am not fine".

He helped me up the stairs, I thanked him, and we both started off our day feeling better for that little exchange.

I also thanked the universe, for giving me the sign that I am not always alone.

Get clear on what you want.

You may be reading this chapter thinking, it's alright for some, but I have never known what I wanted, I still don't. I'm not ambitious. I lead a simple life. I don't have huge dreams or desires to travel.

In the next chapter, we will look in more detail at how you can get to your soul's true calling, but for now I would suggest simply having a playful and adventurous approach to working out what your BFSG should be.

Being able to write a list of things you want to experience without any pressure to even enjoy them or have them lead to anything more than just a one off interesting experience feels exciting.

How to get what you want

Remember as a child when you literally wanted EVERYTHING?

I find it quite joyous watching my daughter get excited at children's TV adverts with calls of:

"I want that mummy... and that... and that, oh and I really want that".

Now, of course she doesn't get any of it, or rarely does. I just love how she is so clearly able to express her desires. There is nothing wrong with asking for what you want.

I remember she came home from a weekend with her dad and she said to me:

"Ask don't get." I was like, "WHAT????"

And she told me that her nan, or her dad, or someone had said that in response to her asking for something.

Now I get the sentiment of that - especially if she had been rude, or was having a tantrum or something (which can happen), but I hated that she had remembered the phrase so clearly, and I was determined for it not to be a phrase that she thought to be true.

I want her to believe that anything is possible, and that anything she wants can be hers.

Which is very different from giving her everything she wants, very different.

One Christmas when she was three years old, all she wanted was some disposable nappies for her dollies. I had bought her loads of other stuff, but she kept going on about them, so the day before Christmas I headed to the shops to get some.

£4.99!!!

They wanted almost a fiver for three pretend nappies. I could have got a pack of the real ones for about the same price.

I put them down and attempted to leave the shop.

Of course then the guilt sank in.

It was the only thing she wanted.

On Christmas day when she opened that gift you would have thought it was the most expensive gift she had received. That £5 gift her gave her so much joy it was unreal. In fact two years later she still has those disposable nappies (the stickers don't stick) and she takes great pride in packing them and unpacking them in her dolls bag.

You deserve to get what you want too.

Not something close to what you want. Not something similar...or as good as. You should be able to get exactly the thing you ask for and know what it feels like to be fulfilled.

Being able to ask and receive is a fundamental part of knowing your worth and living a life full of adventure.

So let's start pinning some of that down.

Check & Challenge 63 – Create a 100 list

A fun activity for working out what you want is to create a 100 list.

This is basically a list of 100 things you want.

When I do this exercise with women they either:

- Run off and have great fun

Or

- Sit there scratching their head with about five things on the list

The thing with this list is that things on it can be big or small, insignificant or massively poignant, they can be expensive or cheap, hard to come by or pedestrian. The trick is to literally listen to your soul and not judge yourself for anything that goes on the list.

So give it a go, write 100 things you truly want and then tick them off as you attract them into your life. If you are really brave you will share your list, or items from your list, with the people you love.

In the next chapter, I will share with you the power of releasing these desires into the world, and to prove to you just how powerful this list can be, here is a selection of some of the things which have been on my 100 list over the last three years that I have indeed ticked off it now.

1. Do stand-up comedy
2. Win an award
3. Speak abroad
4. Do a Tedx talk
5. Fly first class
6. Start a monthly podcast
7. Have my mum see me speak
8. Join a speaking mastermind
9. Do an ultra-marathon
10. Go to a private members club
11. Get life insurance
12. Get teeth sorted (braces)
13. Create own video studio at home
14. Eat in a Michelin Star Restaurant
15. Go to a hot spa
16. Do CrossFit
17. Do a Disney race
18. Visit a fortune teller
19. Do an Olympic Distance Triathlon
20. Go up the Shard
21. Hire a stylist
22. Get funding from Sport England
23. Get my eyebrows micro bladed
24. Be the closing keynote speaker at a conference
25. Climb a mountain

A few I have in the pipeline:

26. Run the New York Marathon
27. Spend the summer in Bali
28. Do a yoga course
29. Do a two-day ultramarathon

And for true transparency, and a nod to my belief that if you put it out there it makes it easier for the universe to provide, here are some that I am still holding out for:

30. Be invited to 10 Downing Street
31. Become a Hay House Author
32. Get married
33. Be mortgage free
34. Write a novel
35. Meet Richard Branson

Your list will of course look different to mine, and so it should. You get to decide what you want, and remember you don't get to decide on what anyone else should or shouldn't want.

So don't judge me.

It's worth noting that when I first started doing my 100 list, I thought it was the most ridiculous, self-serving, pie-in-the-sky activity ever.

I didn't ever think any of these things would ever happen to me, but once I saw that some of these things were possible, it helped me to dream even bigger and start to believe that I was worthy of having nice things and nice experiences in my life, because these things were symbolic of other forces much bigger than me.

Curating a life full of adventure doesn't have to be about ticking things off your list, it can be about filling your life with fun, laughter, connection, learning, giving, sharing...you make of it what you want.

That is the glory of life, right?

Bigger Than You

Are you ready yet to accept who you truly are?
And then share that more with the world?

When I was eight years old, I started collecting rubbers or erasers - you know the things you use with pencils, not the things that come in a box of three...anyway I had heaps of them. I think it was a craze back then, perhaps it still is now among girls of that age.

Around the age of 10, I had a brief interest in collecting stamps from around the world (I think someone had offloaded their own small collection to me) but you couldn't do much with them other than look at them.

Then at 14 years old, life got really exciting when I started collecting quotes.

Please remember people, this was the mid-1990s, the internet was not quite a thing yet and we didn't have memes with inspirational slogans. Shit man, we didn't even have cable TV at home, therefore couldn't access the wise words of Oprah Winfrey even if we wanted to.

The closest we had to a life coach on our screens in the UK was Trisha Goddard from the Trisha Show (remember her?) or the national treasure that was Esther Rantzen - neither of whom I could really relate to if I am being honest.

Somehow I would stumble across these inspirational quotes from people I didn't even know anything about, and I would scribble their wise words down or cut them out of magazines and add them to my diary for the year (journal was a term I would come to at least 10 or 15 years later)

One which really struck me was from American actress, Mae West, who said:

"Better to be looked over than overlooked."

I lived by that motto for the longest time.

It has meant many things to me through the years. In my teens, it meant... let them stare, they are just jealous. In my 20s, it meant... you might not be everyone's cup or tea, but still keep putting yourself out there. In my 30s, it meant...be visible, people will take strength from you showing up the way you do.

And now???

It mainly means I have a job to do while I am here on this planet, and it involves showing up every day 100% as me.

I truly believe that we are put on this planet for a purpose.

All of us.

I think it is part of our evolutionary journey, that very much like the film The Matrix everything is connected, and that our behaviours affect each other in ways we don't always understand.

I know that some of us are more open to ideas like this, and that it can sometimes feel weird to believe that "little ole you" has anything of value to contribute to this big old world.

You can't deny though when you look back at your own family history and reflect on how Uncle Bob raised eight children by himself in a two-up, two-down in Yorkshire or Great-granny Mary's achievements in engineering, that in years to come, someone will be doing this with regards to you. By the time you die, you will have influenced hundreds of people, maybe thousands, and that the world will be different as a result of those interactions.

Surely that in and of itself is evolution, right?

But what if, by holding yourself back and not being the best version of yourself, you are doing the world an injustice?

Now don't worry if you are all like:

"But what the hell is my purpose?"

It doesn't have to be something big like finding a cure for a tropical disease, or putting an end to world poverty, but deep down you know there is a cause or a belief system that is important to you.

This could be raising a family, or it could be doing charity work. It could be something that we would like to do more of, if we didn't have to work or have other life commitments that kept getting in the way.

For some of us our work is our calling, where our careers are literally the things which enable us to fulfil our purpose.

I have always been lucky that my career path has been dictated by my passions and interests. I've always been interested in people, I've always been drawn to injustice and making the world fairer, and I've always wanted to be able to retell stories through creativity.

The only job I ever did that didn't have much of that going on was when I was a policy manage for a couple of years, and that job literally made me ill. It created disease and unease in my body and my soul, and I thank my lucky stars that I was made redundant when I was - although at the time it was a bitter pill to swallow.

Check & Challenge 64 – What is your purpose?

In one paragraph, have a go at writing what your life's purpose is.

Remember it doesn't have to be career-orientated, it could be about your role as a mother, or your role in the community, or within a cause. Or it can be more about reaching your potential.

Then give this statement a percentage score of how much you are living towards this purpose? Think back to the Living a Bigger Life Quadrant if that helps.

If you don't think you have a purpose, don't fear. We are going to get to the bottom of that next.

Finding your why?

One of the most fundamental questions we can ask is that of why? It's why young children use it so frequently, as they seek to understand the world they are growing into. As adults, though, do we ask ourselves why enough?

Why do I get out of bed?
Why do I go to work?
Why do I eat what I eat?
Why do I dress the way I do?
Why do I feel the way I do?
Why do I behave the way I do?

Trust me if something is out of whack in your life, if something feels off, it only takes a few why questions to get to the bottom of it.

Another question I am fond of is:

What if there was a different way?

I am a rebel, I don't like being told what to do or how to do anything. I like to make sense of things in my own way and act accordingly.

If I can't understand the reasoning behind doing something I won't do it.

And if it doesn't fit with my personal values, I won't either.

But what are my personal values? And why do you need to get yourself some?

"If you don't stand for something you will fall for anything"

This is such a popular expression that many in history have claimed it as their own, everyone from Alexander Hamilton, to Malcom X, Peter Marshall, to Irene Dunne.

It doesn't really matter who said it first, the important thing is we hold on to its sentiment.

In this day and age, there are so many things to fall for.

You can spend your life being pulled from pillar to post, believing in the stuff that people shout loudest about. Just think about all of that misinformation in Chapter 4 about diets. Who do you believe?

Your values are like a set of attitudes or principles that indicate a commitment to act in a certain way, particularly during times of adversity. They can help act as a compass to guide you and to help you make the right decisions, particularly when the answer is not straightforward.

The Red Cross, for example, has seven humanitarian principles that it uses to guide the actions of its aid workers around the world. Meanwhile, the Hippocratic Oath is a very well-known set of values that doctors agree to in order to protect their patient's best interests.

So what are my personal values?

1. Fairness
2. Adventure
3. Humour
4. Respect
5. Progress

And why do these things matter to me?

They are who I am at my core.

Maybe not in every single thing I do, I'm not a bloody saint all of the time.

But they are absolutely the things which I strive for.

They are things I've always believe in, things which have always motivated me.

In 1987, aged nine and a half, I set up a library in the attic room in our house. I devised this venture so I could make new friends, so I could feel important, so I could do something productive over the summer holidays. And also so I could surround myself in the things which I loved most at nine and a half: books.

I got all the books I could find from our house and asked all the kids down my road to borrow (well OK steal) the books from their homes too. I categorised them all and then issued library cards to any of the kids that wanted one. I had encyclopedias, a pop-up section, cushions to lay on and read, and even a rubber stamp...oh how I loved my rubber stamp.
A few years later, I started a kid's club in our garden shed, and we held meetings after school and in the holidays. We would do litter patrol on our estate and knock on old people's doors to ask if they needed any help with shopping or tasks around the house.
The great thing about hair-brained ideas that you have as kids is that you don't have anyone to talk you out of them. You have no expectations, you don't know what is possible, or what the rules are.

You just have a go and see if they will work. When did we lose that?

Is it time for you to take action on your ideas?

Ever have a brilliant idea pop into your head that is super-inspiring and exciting, and maybe even a bit scary? But you know it is something you really want to do?

But then...

You start playing out all of the tasks that lay ahead of you to achieve the goal, and before
you know it you have talked yourself out of it, telling yourself it was a silly idea anyway?

Sound familiar?

The thing is, anything worth having in this life normally takes a bit of work, requiring time, effort, resources, information. It is never straightforward, and for that reason, big life changing plans can feel overwhelming, scary and complex.

It is no wonder we stay in our comfort zone.

But what if we made a deal with our self to just take the very first step, with no pressure, no
expectation, no concern about the steps after that? What if we just took action of the very first thing on the list and dealt with the rest of it at a later date?

Would that be super scary?

When I signed up for the London Marathon back in 2011 I could barely run to the top of my road. If I had worried about a training plan, the right trainers to wear, how to fuel, the fact I'd have to train with other people, the chaffing, the pain, the fatigue... well, I would never have got round to running that race - and my life would be so much different to where I am now.

When I look back at all of the significant achievements in my life, I can trace each and every one of them back to some kind of mundane reasonably pedestrian step - an action that often required something as simple as saying yes to an opportunity, typing my details into a website or handing over my credit card.

Don't for a moment think I am minimalising the effort it requires to take the first step.
It is scary, it takes courage, it requires a massive leap of faith.

But that phase between courage and confidence only needs to last a moment.

And it requires just one thing: COMMITMENT!!!

Make the decision, and then rip the band-aid off with inspired action until the fear leaves you, until the pain of potential failure disappears under the excitement of new challenge.

The 6 Steps to Greatness

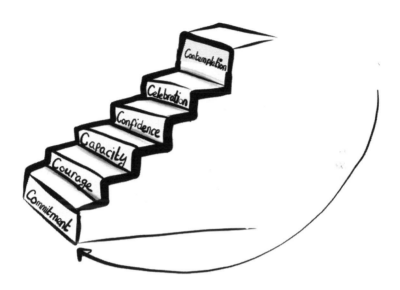

Having a process for achieving your goals which involves the inclusion of external forces such as public accountability and a commitment to sharing your successes and struggles is critical to actually moving forward in your life.

When you enable other people to buy into your goals, they become bigger than you and they build momentum. In some ways, when you do this, you turn this diagram on its head and its almost like you are running down the stairs instead, building momentum with each step.

Commitment is the first step for sure.

Go up those stairs not down. Don't spend too long contemplating. Start by committing, and then getting on with the job at hand.

Over the years I have got better and better at taking these first steps. I find it easier to identify them, to act on them more promptly and to appreciate their power.

It has helped me channel my fear and kick-start some incredible adventures. It has helped many of the women in my Living a Bigger Life coaching programme change their lives and achieve their goals, and it could do exactly the same for you.

Try not to stress about the hows, and focus instead on the whys and the feeling of accomplishment at each step.

Check & Challenge 65 – Sketch out your path to greatness one step at a time

Using the diagram above as a guide and sketch out your Big Fat Stupid Goal, or even one of your smaller goals such as something from your 100 things.

Still struggling to pin down some goals?

Let's get those juices flowing, with a fabulous exercise which taught me how to dream.

Be. Do. Have

The Spice Girls were really on to something in the early 90s. Like really on to something. As much as we mock them and joke about their light-hearted pop songs and their crazy outfits, they really did shake things up.

In my view, their song "Wannabe" is one of the best girl-band songs of all times. It is a feminist anthem reminding men that we are in control and I just simply love the simplicity of the lyrics:

"I tell you what I want, what I really really want" and then the ever confusing "zig-a-zig- ah".

The fact is that so many women don't know what they want.

Not really.

One of my favourite exercises for working out what you want is a coaching tool called The Be Do Have model, which the business strategists, Stephen Covey and Anthony Robbins, have used in their writing, although I believe it predates both of them.

It is a wonderfully powerful framework for lasting change and helps you to dream and visualise the world you want for yourself, and, equally important, what you don't want.

I first did this exercise in 2013.

I now do it at least two or three times a year, to see if anything has shifted, and to remind myself of what is important to me.

I'm not going to lie to you, it took a few times to truly be honest with me and cut out the bullshit. And some of what I wrote scared the living daylights out of me. I admitted to things I had desired for a long time, but didn't want to own up to because secretly I didn't think they were within my grasp.

Ultimately, I didn't believe I was worthy of them. These tools helped me to do the mindset work I needed to do to shift those stories.

Check & Challenge 66 – What do you want to be, do and have?

Fill in this table and be as honest as you can about what you desire. Don't judge yourself, and do not obsess about how realistic any of it is.

Have a look back at the list of values you wrote for yourself back in Chapter 5 to help guide you.

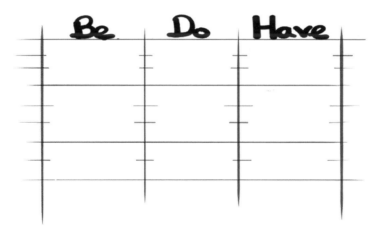

Becoming who you were meant to be

It has taken me some time to get to the point in my life where I have this level of self awareness and clarity on what I want from life.

This work is ongoing. It's not like you can read a self-help book about being the best version of yourself, or go on a seminar of some kind to learn your self-limiting beliefs and then be all like "I'm fixed!!!"

As we grow and evolve as people, our thinking must grow and evolve too. In many ways I wish I had come to this place much sooner in my life as it would have saved much heart ache.

I don't particularly enjoy writing about my relationship breakdown with my daughters' father, but much of our problems came from our inability to understand one another, and the fact that we actually wanted different things from life.

Therefore, we were unable to fulfill each other. The compromise was too great and so what ensued was a power struggle.

Looking back, it is easy to see that when I met him I was desperately lonely, looking for someone to take care of me, and I was willing to give up almost everything for that.

I was absolutely in a place of fear:

- Fear of being alone forever
- Fear of never being a mother
- Fear of never finding love

I will always be grateful for the things that relationship taught me about love, and who I am in a relationship. That relationship changed the path of my life indefinitely. So I will never look back on it with regret.

Ultimately, it put me on a trajectory of self-discovery, and enabled me to really work out who I am and what it is I am looking for in life - and I guess from a potential future partner too.

The real discovery though was who I would become in my new role as mother.

Everything changed the moment I had a daughter. Not just a child, but specifically a daughter.

I had a lot of time to think things through when Rose arrived. I had been made redundant from my job a few months before she arrived, and it would be close to a year before I started any kind of meaningful work again.

Lots of time to think.

To think about my relationship with my parents. To think about the kind of mother I wanted to be. The kind of child I wanted to raise. Nothing quite prepared me for the sense of responsibility I would feel as a parent. Not

228

necessarily to do things right (there is enough pressure to be the perfect parent), but instead to do things in a way that felt right to me.

I realised probably as little as six months into being a mum that I couldn't be the mother I needed to be for Rose, or the woman I needed to be for me, while still being in a relationship with her dad.

It took me another two years to build up the courage to finally end the relationship, and a further two years to get to a place where I was 100% sure that it was the right thing to do.

The bottom line was I was not happy in that relationship, I wasn't fulfilled.

I knew I was not able to be my true authentic self, and in many ways because of my values and belief system, I wasn't enabling my then partner to be his best self either. And our beautiful daughter was stuck in the middle of this.

She deserved better.

I deserved better.

He deserved better.

Even if that meant for all of us it got a bit worse before it could get a bit better. But I have no regrets. It was the right thing to do.

During the hardest moments of those years I had to remind myself repeatedly that I deserved happiness too. That it was OK for me to want a life filled with adventure, self-fulfillment and joy.

This did not make me a bad person.

I knew this because I knew in years to come I would be trying to teach my daughter about valuing herself, and prioritising her health and happiness. How could I do that with any authority if I had put my happiness to one side for the sake of someone else's idea of what constituted a family?

I knew that despite the emotional and practical mess that was our relationship breakup I would eventually get to a point where we would all come out winners, even if I was completely shitting myself at the time about what a mess I had made of my life.

Using fear as a barometer

People often say to me...

"Julie, you are fearless."

I am not fearless. I am fearful every single day of my life. But do you know what? Even though I still experience fear. I no longer fear fear. And that is the greatest relief.

Through my life and especially in the past five years I have been through so much heartbreak, disappointment and despair, that I have learned just how capable I am to overcome most things.

And that fear of the future, that fear of the unknown is just an unnecessary factor, that stopped me from moving forward in my life.

When I was in the midst of indecision and confusion over how to move forward after finding myself unemployed and a single mum, I reminded myself that the only thing I had to fear was the place I had just come from, and there was no way I was ever going back there.

These days, I choose to use fear as a barometer, as a check and challenge measure to work out what I want and what I don't in my life, highlighting the actions I need to take to move me further towards or away from the things that are important to me.

Look ladies, it is simply impossible to have a life full of adventure without fear, so we have to make friends with fear and not avoid it at any cost. When we admit to our self that we have resistance to something, it helps us identify what those fears really are.

Being scared of going to the gym is often about the fear of judgement, or the fear of losing control.

Similarly in regards to public speaking, it is not the audience we are afraid of; it is what is going on in their heads that is the problem. Worrying about what a bunch of complete strangers may or may not think about you - much like when I did my TEDx. I couldn't control what people thought of me, I just had to trust that my message would get to who I needed it, that there would be a payoff.

None of us want to put ourselves forward to be ridiculed or critiqued, but what alternative do we have? Hide away?

We have to learn to stand up and be seen, exactly as we are.

That is what true courage looks like.

So get practicing.

Get into the habit of not only asking "what is the worst that could happen?", but "what is the best?"

There can be negative consequences of doing well for yourself and achieving your goals, which can inadvertently stop us from acting on our goals.

For example, a typical thought process about a new idea might go like this...

Do you know what I'd love to do?
I'd love to launch a business that did X,Y & Z
I think people would really buy into that.
I would have to leave my job, and work from home.
I'd be able to see more of the kids and work more flexibly.
If all worked out well I could build a team.
Have people working for me.
The money could be really good.
There would be travel too, I love to travel.
It could build me the kind of life I've always dreamed off.
But what about my friends, they all have normal jobs.
I might start making more money than them, and might have to pay for them sometimes.
People might start asking to borrow money from me.
People might try and take advantage of me.
The kids will become brats and want everything handed to them on a plate.
My husband won't be the main breadwinner.
People will think I am greedy, and selfish, and have got to big for my boots.
Maybe I don't deserve that kind of lifestyle.
More money more problems right?
Maybe I will just stick to my job after all.
Its not that bad.

Sound familiar?

Calling out your internal bullshit is a real skill. Once you know how to do this though, there is no going back. Once a fear is named, it loses its power in my mind. Giving these thoughts a name almost forces them to shut the fuck up.

"Ah, that's just my self-limiting beliefs talking there."

"Oh give it a rest Resistance, I'm gonna do it anyway."

"Give me a break Fear, I had enough of you yesterday."

Check & Challenge 67 - Who wins when you win?

Write a list of the people who win when you win. Who will benefit when you achieve your goal? Think about those close to you, but also those that are watching from afar, and those who will be impacted by the things you do in this world, long after you have gone.

When we reach our full potential, we model what that looks like to others and it encourages them to live their biggest boldest self too.

It isn't always easy to find role models of women being successful in their own right.

Women who are living life by their own set of rules.

Women who make no apology for themselves.

We need to see more of that in this world.

I was the first woman to go to university from my family. There have since been others, and that whole world has now been opened to my nieces and nephews, who perhaps otherwise wouldn't have had any reference point to call upon.

Now I can't single handedly claim I have influenced every single overweight runner in the world to take up running, but what I do know for sure is that my work with Too Fat to Run over the past eight years has absolutely changed the landscape of running for women, and has had influence in the sports world in ways I will never truly understand.
Every time I posted a picture of me in my Lycra with my lumps and bumps hanging out, I was showing other women that this was an option for them too.

What Lycra taught me about visibility

Lycra is a strange old fabric which kind of gets a bad press really.

Because, even if it isn't the most flattering of materials, Lycra is integral to your enjoyment of sport - plus you try finding pants that stay up without it!!!

When I first started running more than 15 years ago, I went out in cotton tracksuit bottoms, a t-shirt and a pair of Reebok classics. I didn't know any better. Gosh, if I ever tried to re-enact that there outfit now I doubt I would get to the top of my road without the quality of the fabric getting on my nerves. When I run now, I wear tight fitting Lycra running leggings, even in my lumpy, bumpy size-18 body. I put on those bad boys and I hit the streets without a care in the world because I couldn't give a flying fart what other people think of me when I am out running.

Long gone are those days where I run after dark or in secluded backstreets for fear of being seen. I am loud and proud now. The wearing of Lycra in my plus-size body has taught me a lot about being seen over the years, lessons which I think are absolutely transferable to life and to business.

So here are four of the lessons that Lycra has so kindly taught me visibility:

1. **Hiding your imperfections only draws attention to them**
   Have you ever noticed a person on the beach on a really hot day covered head to toe in clothes because they think the sight of them in a swimsuit will draw attention to them? The thing is, the curious mind in all of us makes them a target as you try to work out their story. The truth is on a beach and in life, people are normally so preoccupied with thoughts of their own insecurities, they barely register those around you. And if they do clock you...? See below.

2. **Those who matter don't mind, and those who mind don't matter**
   I have spent my whole life being heckled. While out running in my plus-size body, I am a bit of a target. However, these heckles are not always restricted to when I am out training. People somehow find the need to shout out all kinds of stuff in all manner of places. What I learned from this though is I am never going to stop showing up as me, and if that means wearing tight-fitting clothes to play sport or red shoes to go dancing then so be it. I have turned up to really important meetings in my running kit, appeared on national TV, and given talks to 1000s of people in Lycra, knowing that they can see all of my lumps and bumps, because I have an important message to share. Just because I don't look like you average runner, doesn't mean I need to hide away. If my lumps and bumps are what they are focusing on, then that says more about me than it does them.

3. **People respect openness and honesty**
   In a world where everything is photo-shopped and styled to within an inch of its life, I think most of us find seeing someone in their true state kind of refreshing. A glossy Instagram feed and a different designer handbag each day doesn't make me want to work with someone – besides, it's never possibly to tell whether this is all fake. The more you can show up without the crutches of perceived perfection, the more people will want to be around you. Don't get me wrong, I am all for

making an effort, having your nails done, wearing nice clothes when appropriate, but nobody can look perfect and polished 100% of the time. There is nothing more empowering and bonding than a big bunch of women red-faced and sweaty after a race - add to that some mud and you are on to an absolute winner.

4. **Your body is an important part of your story**
Of course people make snap judgments about you based on your appearance, but regardless of this, you get to choose how you treat it. Our bodies in many ways tell a story, and by embracing and unlocking the confidence to accept, understand or even share your story, it becomes easier to change that story or boldly embrace it, whichever you chose. Oprah Winfrey in her glorious speech at the Golden Globes said, *"Speaking your truth is the most powerful tool you have"* – **which** is why I am not a big fan of those hold me in pants. Let it all hang out, I say.

It scares me that so many teenage girls drop out of sport because of the irrational fear of being seen in fitness clothes.

It worries me that in the business world women hold themselves back because they feel like they have to have the perfect hair, the perfect smile, the perfect backdrop to show up on things like Facebook Live or YouTube.

My experience working with women shows me this increases significantly when women are overweight or dissatisfied with their bodies or the way they look.

It saddens me that women hold back from pursuing new relationships thinking they will wait until they have lost weight, or have a better wardrobe to woo a future mate.

If trusting relationships are based on us being open, and being able to look each other in the eye, surely we are putting our self at a disadvantage by not showing up fully as ourselves, by hiding aspects of our self away?

Life is far too short to be held back by fears about how you look, especially when you have so much to offer this world outside of all that. What you look like does not define who you are.

Are you showing up in your own life?
Are you being visible?
Are you hiding?
Is it time to step from behind the curtain?
Time to stand up for something?

234

Time to speak out more?
Is it time for you to be more visible?
Is it time for you to picture what this new life would look and feel like?

We are now approaching the final chapter of this book, the moment where you literally have to put this down and start doing the bleeding work. I'm thinking about the journey we have been on together, the distance we have covered, and of course the stuff that we have uncovered.

Have we come up with any answers?

Are we any closer to working out what a BIGGER life looks like for us? Are we enough yet? Are we feeling like we want more? Or are we desperate to simplify? Are we ready to stand up, to speak out, to move forward?

Are we willing, ready and able to take inspired action? Is it time for action now?

If we are ready to take that important leap of faith to make significant changes in our lives, we have to at least be able to see where we are heading. Because isn't that part of the problem? We can't imagine ourselves doing those exciting things, being that different, more adventurous person? We need to be able to see the path. It doesn't have to be the whole path, but at least some kind of reminder that this new way of being is worth the effort.
Because it isn't going to be plain sailing. You are going to want to go back to your old ways, and find that warm and familiar place that is your comfort zone.

It's time to start visualizing, time to create a shrine.

Check & Challenge 68 - Create a shrine to your new life

When the daily grind of work, family life and other responsibilities get us down, we need some way to remind ourselves of what we are working towards. A daily reminder to STOP, review and then take action in the right way, rather than going with the flow and just firefighting your way through life.

For me, there is one activity that helps me do this over and above anything else, and that is through the power of visualization.

How can I move towards what I want if I can't see it?

The answer?

You have to literally paint a picture, so that you can imagine what it would look like when you get there, and then use those images as a way of evoking the feelings you will feel when it is yours.

I like to create a vision board for this, but you may want to use Pinterest, or a pinboard, or have an area in your home that acts as a shrine to the life you are working towards. You can be as visible with this as you like, or instead choose small symbolic signs as a daily prompt to evoke those feelings.

The main goal is to be reminded every single day of your desire to live bigger.

Being the Bestest Version of You

This is it...warts and all, take it or leave it. This is me

So here we are my friend. We have arrived at the end of this book. I don't know about you but I could do with a cuppa. A cuppa and a fortnight in the Maldives...heck I'd settle for a weekend in an Air B&B apartment with Netflix and a massive bar of Galaxy...something to signal me finally reaching the end of this book.

But this is not the end. We are not done yet.

Because this is the start of our adventure. Where we take up arms and become the warriors we know we can be.

We pause.

We take a breath.

We reflect.

And then we make a plan.

Let me ask you something? Have you ever get to a point in your life where you literally ask...How the hell did I end up here?

Where you think about all the external forces, and happenings, coincidences and choices personal and world matters that have coincided to get you to the point in the world where you are today?

It can be overwhelming.

But it can also be a really useful tool to take stock and be grateful.

I do this all the time, I sit and just think about everything and everyone that came before me to make me who I am. I know it sounds dramatic, you may even question how I have time for that shit.

But I do.

I know other women do too.

This is the stuff of life. It is about evolution. Our future as human beings, and yet so often we are afraid to think so deeply because in many ways we feel powerless to inflict change anyway, so what's the point?

I find this kind of contemplation generally happens when either really really good stuff happens in your life, or when you have hit absolute rock bottom….and sometimes when you are forced to admit that this planet we live on is a pretty epic place.

Do you find that?

Like the rest of the time we are blinkered, and just dealing with the day to dayness of life to really think about this kind of stuff. Yet take us to a pretty beach, half way up a mountain, or to some kind of sacred space…and it almost allows us to step away from our humdrum lives for a moment and just dream, ponder, escape.

Check & Challenge 69 – How did you REALLY get here?

Spend an afternoon looking at old photos, reading letters, studying your family tree. Read up on the women's movement, watch movies about strong women from history. Think about your place in all of that and be thankful that you are here as you are.

I often have these moments that remind me somewhat of the Matrix - where all of a sudden everything seems crystal clear, when I am in the zone, like everything makes sense.

For me, this clarity often happen when I am running in a different country, or climbing up a mountain, or attending a posh event somewhere being recognised for my work. It happens when I get off the phone from an awesome client, or when I wave my ladies off from another emotional retreat. It happened recently as I watched my brother get married, and on holiday with Rose in moments of real unreserved joy.

I ask myself: "How did this happen?"

"How have I come so far?"

This year I turned 40.

Four Zero…I know, I know. Forty whole years on this planet. Four Decades… How is that even possible?

For context, this means when I was born, the following things had not been invented yet:

- Selfies and selfiesticks
- Wikipedia
- Google
- Fitness trackers
- Fruit pouches
- Febreeze
- Facebook
- Prozac

How did we cope?

Now if that doesn't make you feel old.

It's funny. When I was a teenager I thought that by the time I hit 40 I would have my life all figured out: I'd be happily married, in a proper job, couple of kids on the go, a house I owned, a couple of holidays a year, maybe a semi-decent car, definitely a tidy wardrobe and matching crockery. Wow, I didn't want much, did I?

I didn't want much at all in fact.

My life at 40 doesn't look like that at all really, and I'm not that fussed. I think the biggest revelation from having hit that big milestone earlier this year is that although I still feel relatively young, I still don't feel much like an adult yet.

- I hate washing up
- I don't like ironing clothes
- I hate having to make big decisions
- I hate having to read maps (or follow the Sat Nav)
- I can't do flat-pack furniture
- I still don't understand the off side rule
- Boys still stink
- And I still begrudge paying for toilet paper

I wonder if any of that will ever change.

There has been one big shift though that I wasn't quite expecting.

Other women warned me it was coming, but I wasn't too sure.

The big revelation?

I don't actually care what people think of me anymore.

I know that sounds flippant, and maybe I should care what some people think....
Maybe I do when it is people I love and respect, or where I need to make a good impression for work or something.

But generally speaking, for people I don't know, who will probably play no role in my life...
I couldn't give a flying fuck.

And trust me I used to... Oh how I used to. Every internet troll's comment, every Daily Mail article, every negative book review, every "but running should be free" email, I used to make it all so personal. Somehow I don't really hear any of that unnecessary noise now - and it's amazing.

My fear of judgment is minuscule compared to what it used to be.
Because there was a time where I second-guessed everything because I was absolutely crippled by the fear of people thinking badly of me.

I was so critical about how I looked, and not only about my weight but my height, my teeth, my freckles, the mole on my face, my slightly wonky nose, my frizzy hair, my hit and miss dress sense... The list was endless.

That list was exhausting.

Often what people think has nothing to do with you, and everything to do with the person judging you.

It is their shit.
It is the crap they hold in their heads and their hearts
The toxic mess that in many ways affects them even more than it affects us.

We all know what it is to judge someone unfairly, and in the moment we might take a little joy from it, but deep down we know it cuts into us somewhere, somehow too, right?

We are not what we look like.

Our bodies are simply the vessels that carry our soul. It is not our duty as women to be beautiful. Unless you are a model or a movie star who is playing the part of someone of undeniable beauty, you have permission to go about your business looking exactly as you do. Make up or no make up, hair brushed or not, latest fashion, or clothes from the market, it doesn't matter.

It doesn't dictate your value as a woman.

I'm all for making the most of what you have, I like wearing nice clothes (sometimes) and having my nails done as much as the next woman, but this pursuit of perfection on top of the exhausting pursuit of smallness is just soul destroying.

And the reality is, even with all the will in the world, a wonderful stylist and extensive surgery, my looks are unlikely to change much anyway.

NO MORE!!!

We can change the world or we can focus on making our self look better. We ain't got the time or energy to do both... Well, I haven't anyway.

Know what I mean?

Surely the most important person to impress is yourself right?

And if not impress, then surely at least we should accept who we are and be OK with it.

As I prepared for my TEDx talk earlier this year about showing up unapologetically as yourself, I realised just how consumed I have been in my life with that fear of judgment. I reflected on the number of missed opportunities and slightly ruined experiences because I was worried about how I looked or what strangers might or might not think of me.

Crying over blokes who were mean to me in bars or girls who made bitchy comments. I'd spend weeks analysing a comment or a look given by someone where I couldn't quite work out its intent, always jumping to the negative outcome first.

I knew the moment I stood on that stage I would be judged, and there was nothing I could do about it. In fact, 10 minutes before I was due on stage I managed to squirt foundation on my crisp white blouse. But instead of freaking out, I simply laughed. I felt like it was a sign, a sign to remind me of my message.

Luckily I had a spare. Also, in that moment I decided to go onto that stage in the cheap Primark jeans I'd been wearing all day, rather than the fresh expensive pair I had bought especially for the occasion.

It was my two fingers up to what people thought of me gesture, even if I was the only person who knew I was doing it.

Judgment is simply a human trait.
Nothing more, nothing less. We must not let it define us.
I am done with living my life to please other people.
I have got important shit to do.
You do too.

Ten years ago, I almost didn't continue with the sport I now love, an activity which has helped me to start a movement for the good of others. Why? Because some little kid shouted "Run Fatty Run" and all his mates laughed, and because yet again I came dead last in a race and found the finish line gone.

Those things were a test for me. I believe those things happened as a wake-up call.
As a call to action. Not to get fitter, faster and to lose some weight, but to embark on a journey of self-acceptance.

And it is 100% a journey.

It is not like you are going to wake up one day and never care what anyone thinks of you ever again. It's not like all of a sudden you are going to find the inner strength to come from within your comfort zone and do a bunch of incredible stuff forever more.

It is a process.

A muscle that needs building. ·

I believe as women we need to wake up each day and climb inside one of those big inflatable zorbing balls. You know the things people throw themselves down hills in for fun?

We need to climb into one of those each day, safe in the knowledge that we can't be hurt by the comments, views or opinions of others we encounter. Where we can metaphorically (or literally if you want...just add it to your 100 list) roll down the hill of life having an absolute blast, blissfully unaware of all the crap outside of your sphere.

We have to do that for our self.
Perhaps we shouldn't have to but for now we do.
We must be more resilient.
We must be more aware of our reactions and interactions.
We must be more willing to take action on the things that matter.
We must question the status quo.

And we must call out injustice when we see it - even if that injustice is only affecting us in a small way. It is those micro aggressions, those micro annoyances, those micro restraints that keep us from doing our important work.

We have to find a way of being able to stay on our path and not be blindsided by the foolishness that surround us, we have to find a way of being able to switch off and be unfazed by it.

A time to reflect

Some 100 years ago, on February 6th 1918 to be exact, the UK parliament passed the Representation of the People Act - the act of parliament that enabled women to vote for the first time.

This year we marked this centenary with all manor of events, talks, films and celebrations, and it helped me as a woman to reflect on the journey we have been on to stand up and be counted in this world.

However, for an unmarried, working class girl like me it would have been a further 10 years before I would have been allowed to vote as the original act wasn't for all women. Let's not forget that some countries were even further behind the UK. It blows my mind that it took until 1994 for South African women to get the vote, 2005 for Kuwait, 2011 for Saudi Arabia.

Our fight for equality is far from over.

You know, I never would have considered myself a feminist until recent years. I was naive in thinking that my struggle was just one due to the circumstances I had been born into rather than the gender I happened to be, and that with hard work and determination I could overcome anything.

When I became a mother, I realised this wasn't the case.

In fact, I probably realised this the moment I was made redundant while seven months pregnant, knowing for the first time in my life I had someone else's welfare to consider other than my own, where hard work and determination wouldn't automatically put me back on par with my male counterparts.

Pardon my French, but my life was fucked!!! And although I didn't completely blame the men in my life, they had for sure played a part in this. What I was most angry at was that I had just let it happen.

I feel embarrassed that I was so naive, so blinkered to the issue, that I hadn't taken the time to read more, to better protect myself, and to understand the fight which had been taking place for so many years on my behalf.

Now I am not going to use this book to start trying to smash the patriarchy – I may save that conversation for another time. But what I can say is that we women have an incredible untapped power to make of this world what we imagine it to be, if only we can find the courage to do it.

Imagine the change that could come if we all lived BIGGER…like tomorrow???? Imagine if we collectively supported one another to live BIGGER? Imagine that?

Sometimes I sit back in amazement at some of the things that I have done. I know I couldn't have done them if it was just about me. I was able to stand up and shout out because I was doing it on behalf of a cause that was bigger than me.

When I started speaking out on behalf of plus-size women, highlighting the inequality that existed in the sports world, and showing just how difficult it was to show up in a larger body, I knew I couldn't just play lip service to that, I had to walk the walk, or run the run so to speak.

I was encouraging women to love and value themselves, and I had to do that myself.

That is the real fight.

Yes, we can go on marches, and attend talks, and join political parties which claim to have our interests at heart. But the single most powerful thing we can do for the empowerment and evolution of women, is to love, accept and value our self.

Our true self.

It is time for what I like to call radical self love.

It takes a while to get your head around it, to practice it daily, to not be deterred by the non believers….and/or to talk yourself out of it. But boy, is it worth it.

It changes EVERYTHING.

Ladies, we need to stop with all the bullshit excuses, decide it is time to stop dieting and start living and then finish that off nicely by getting on our metaphorical soap box to simply say

This is me.

Oh-oh-oh-oh
Oh-oh-oh-oh
Oh-oh-oh-oh
Oh-oh-oh-oh
Oh-oh-oh, oh-oh-oh, oh-oh-oh, oh, oh

(Sorry couldn't help myself)

You know where I am going with this right?

So this is where I simply have to make reference to the single most important film of this year, maybe of my life and more notably the song from the soundtrack that has become somewhat of an anti-bullying anthem for millions of people around the world.

I am of course talking about Keala Settles, "This is Me" from the film, The Greatest Showman.

Can you remember where you were when you first watched that film?

When you first heard that song? I can. I was by myself. I laughed, I cried, I did that weird thing where you smile on the inside. You know what I mean? When your heart does something weird that makes you feel all nice?

Yeah, I did all of that by myself.

You see, I have been single for almost four years.

I don't really have anyone to go to the cinema with other than Rose and that has a tendency to limit what we can watch. However, I love the movies, so a couple of years back I made the decision that if there was a film coming out I really wanted to see, I would just go and watch it by myself.

And so that is what I do. Often on a Friday afternoon, when I am exhausted from a hard week and need to switch off, I head to my local 20-screen cinema and I enjoy a movie by myself.

Nothing prepared me for this one.

Inspired by the imagination of P.T. Barnum who was played by Hugh Jackman, The Greatest Showman is an original musical that celebrates the birth of show business and tells of visionary who rose from nothing to create a spectacle that became a worldwide sensation.

If you haven't seen it go watch it NOW.

It's a story about having a BIG DREAM, but also a story about fear, about shame, about being thrown into the spot light, about connection, and community, about having the tenacity and bravery to show up unapologetically as you.

But also a reminder about what is important, and the careful line we must tread between achieving great things, and throwing it all away by wanting too much, and never feeling satisfied.

This song was written for me, I'm sure. It is an anthem for the world, an anthem for anyone who has ever been made to feel like shit because they were different.

I am not a stranger to the dark
Hide away, they say
'Cause we don't want your broken parts

Those lyrics.

Pure genius.

It's no wonder this song was nominated for an Oscar in 2018 for best song.

Despite not winning, it won the hearts of thousands of people worldwide who could connect to the lyrics or the song, and the narrative from the film.

How often have we felt like we are not welcome, like we don't fit in, like there is no place for us to truly be our self?

I've learned to be ashamed of all my scars
Run away, they say
No one'll love you as you are

That's bullshit. People will love you as you are, but only once you do too.

Our scars are what make us unique, whether physical or psychological they are part of us, they helped shape us, and we can find strength as a result of them.

When the sharpest words wanna cut me down
I'm gonna send a flood, gonna drown them out
I am brave, I am bruised
I am who I'm meant to be, this is me

You are Fat, you are Ugly, you are Stupid.

How those words hurt.

You are a mess, you are fucked up, ha look at you now, not so smart now hey? A single parent, broke and on benefits.

Yes. I might have been broke, but I wasn't broken. Not quite.

You see those things, those things which I thought were flaws were actually assets, they helped me to accept myself, even if I couldn't see it at first.

Sticks and stones, that old playground rhyme that was supposed to make us feel better, really should.

We can only be hurt by words when we allow people to hurt us with them.

We get to choose.

I'm not scared to be seen
I make no apologies, this is me

This is me!!!!

Visibility Rocks
You might not know it, or want to even consider this right now but visibility is absolutely the key for women wanting to make changes in their lives.

We must be seen as women.

If not for us, then for those around us, watching, taking notes on what it is to be a woman. How can we truly make peace with our self if we are still hiding away? We can't start to change, if we can not bear to see who we are right now.

Hiding away.

Still protecting our self from the big bad world.

Check & Challenge 70 – Where and how are you not showing up?

Write a list of all the places where you hide? And a list of all the ways you could be more visible. And each week try out ways of increasing your visibility.

- On social media
- In photographs
- At work
- In your community
- In your business

Remember not to think about what's the worst that could happen? No. Think about what's the best that could happen.

If this book has taught you anything it's that we have a choice.

We get to choose our own adventure.
Is it time for a transformation? No matter how big or small?
Are we settling because of the stories we have been told about what women like us should be doing. Are we living up to other people's expectations? Are we winding down, when really we should be winding up?

I learned a long time ago that nobody is coming to save you, you have to be your own rescue, your own saviour.

But that takes action.

Inspired action.

This doesn't mean you have to do it all alone.

No, no, no.

Find your tribe. Find your people. Find your community. Bring together your army of fellow warriors.

And make some shit happen.

Check & Challenge 71 – Time to commit to Living Bigger

Nothing changes unless we do. So as we literally approach the final few paragraphs of this book, I need to know one thing. What are you going to do differently as a result of reading this book?

Be bold and share your goals, your dreams and/or your inspired action plan by posting on social media using the #iblamejulie hashtag.

Be part of this movement.

Be part of my quest to help millions of women live BIGGER, BOLDER, more adventurous lives.

And no this is not a ploy to sell more books.

Trust me, I used to feel ikky about selling my wares, until a wonderful business coach told me "Selling is serving, by not giving people the opportunity to experience your work you are doing the world a disservice"

So now I ask for what I want.

I encourage women who have benefitted from my words, my thoughts, my coaching, to encourage other women to get involved too.

This is not about me. This is about you. The you that you're going to start putting first. The you that is ENOUGH, that is more than enough.

Check & Challenge 72 – Schedule a day for you

There was a lot to take in over the last few hundred pages or so. I hope I have encouraged you to go to places in your mind and in your soul that you haven't been for a while. Got you thinking about things you perhaps never thought you might.

No doubt it can be scary; it can be emotionally draining.

So I would like you to schedule a day for you. A day to recharge. To reboot. Do with it what you choose, but it must be for you. It must be a chance for you to practice this new you. A day to reflect on who you are and who you could be.

This doesn't have to be an expensive spa or a weekend away, it could literally be a change of scenery, a visit to a local beauty spot, an afternoon in your favourite café or library... Do whatever is going to lift you spirits and alter your mood for the good.

I encourage my clients to schedule these dates into their diaries, as though they were work commitments, as though they were afterschool activities for the kids. Non negotiable. Everything else has to work around them because they have value.

Check & Challenge 73 – Pull your plan together

I will say it again. Nothing changes unless we do. We can't expect your life to change without a bit of effort and forward planning.

Head to **www.juliecreffield.com/LBLresources** and download my 90 day planner.

Don't just think about it. Fill the damn thing in.

Can I be frank?

People read books all the time and take no action on them.

And that's OK.

This is not where I tell you that unless you follow the instructions from this book you will never amount to anything, never live a BIGGER life. That's bullshit, you know it and I know it.

You read the book.
I am grateful that you did.

For a start it means all those hours of sitting at my desk drinking copious amounts of tea and worrying that the world was going to hate me were worth it. Besides some books change you, even when you don't act on them

It's like the films that can't be unwatched.

The art that can't be unseen.

The end is nigh

Coming to the end of this book feels like a massive milestone for me. Unlike any other book I have ever produced. This is me laid bare. Not perfect. Not overly produced. Just me showing up trying to be of service because it is the right thing to do.

A potential client emailed me a few weeks ago and asked,

"If you are writing a book with all of your coaching techniques, why would anyone ever work with you as their coach" Like I was giving away EVERYTHING.

That's all good with me. I am happy to share what I know, the tools and techniques that I do indeed use within some of my programmes. What else am I going to do...keep it all to myself?

They are by no means EVERYTHING.

And of course in this book you don't get me...literally kicking your backside. You don't get my years of experience, or me popping into you day via the power of social media with my FB lives and zoom sessions...or meeting you for tea...I loooovvve meeting my clients for tea.

This book is my gift to the world, it is an outpouring of love and appreciation for where I am, and what I've learned. So hopefully it will be received as so.

I hope you have had moments through this book which have woke you up, that have made you sit up and think, "Do you know what she's right" and has prompted you to take action on things even in just a small way.

I hope you feel driven to share these accomplishments with me, whether publically via social media or privately via email, or if you ever bump into me in real life.

I love to be able to celebrate your wins with you. Your wins, are my wins. Just like mine are yours.

I am inspired every single day by the women I am lucky enough to come into contact with. I will be eternally grateful for the love and support women have shown me as I tried to build back my life when it was in tatters.

This book is for every single woman, who ever did something kind for another woman, without wanting or needing anything in return.

In my life, there have been many of those wonderful women.

I wish I could have read this book when I was 15 years old, believing I was the fattest, ugliest, stupidest girl ever to have been born.

I wish I had read this book when I stupidly thought working hard in my career was enough to build a happy life, or that settling down with the first bloke that really showed any interest in staying with me long term.

I have written the book that I need to read now, just as much as I write it for you.

As a constant reminder that I am great just as I am.

I hope you have happened upon this book at a time where it made sense for you to read it, where it reminds you of your greatness (no matter how hidden) and that you have been inspired to use your talents, your special gifts, your contribution to this world for good, particularly when those things benefit other women on this planet.

There is something shifting for women right now, and it feels bloody great to be a part of it.

Get involved.

Play your part.

Experience this shift.

Please don't spend any more time, money, effort or energy in the pursuit of smallness, we don't need less of you in this world...we need more.

More of your amazingness. More of your uniqueness. We need the real you to show up.

It's time to be brave, my love. It's time to be bold.

To set yourself free.

It's time to set yourself some Big, Fat, Stupid Goals and get out there into the world to start living your BIGGER LIFE.... Exactly as you are.

Because, you are enough.

Always

Julie

Acknowledgements

Words are never enough. Not on their own. And not without action.

As the slogan went during the fight for the womens vote a hundred years ago.

Deeds not words.

People talk a good talk, but they don't always follow through.

However, this book is here in your hands not through words but through actions, inspired action.

These 80,000 or so words happened not only because of me, but also because of the kind and generous actions of a number of women...and a few blokes too, who have given me unwavering support.

Folks who supported me through my toughest times.

Who willed me to do well, to finish the book, to ramp up the movement.

Who saw something in me that I couldn't always see in myself.

Becky Slack my editor and dear friend, you fucking rock.

I have never met such an incredibly talented, beautiful and generous woman. From the moment we met I knew we were going to get on...in fact I think you gave me a bit of a telling off over email and I can remember thinking "She's a pain in the arse but rightly so. I like her"

You helped shape this book under the most annoying of circumstances. Maybe I will write a book like a normal person in the future...with proper deadlines and everything.

You were introduced to me by your friend Jo Franco, another incredible woman I have had the privilege of getting to know over the last few years. Jo thank you. You always give it to me straight. No bullshit. I want to be you when I eventually grow up.

Liza Vallance, Sharon Bradford, Cass Kanti, Sarah Badell...what the hell would I have done without you ladies over the last few years? You have always seen the value in the Too Fat to Run movement and gone over and aboard.

My speaker pals Bryony Thomas, Julie Holmes, Susan J Mumford, Celia Delaney, Maggie Georgopoulos, Mel Sherwood, Pam Burrows, Sharon Ameso, Anis Qizilbash, Heather Waring, Dr Linda Shaw...and too many more to mention, you guys understand all too well this weird world we live in, you encourage me to be me and yet help me keep my ego in check when I need that. (my male speaker buddies too like Alan, Charlie, Andy, Nathan and Jeremy you have been amazing too)

The wonderful business buddies I have in my virtual world...god the shit you have to put up with from me sometimes, especially my business coach Gemma Went so so glad I took a chance on you...and in turn you continue to have my back when things go tits up as they inevitably do in business.

To Kerrie Rycroft, you were simply an angel to me on one of my darkest days some years back. We only knew each other vaguely online and you did something so generous I won't ever forget it. You continue to be a sounding board not only in business but in my life.

To my sister Jennie...I am nothing without your practical support, and your ability to help me live like a proper person. You won't ever let me forget where I came from...why do you think I keep you so close to me ha ha...I can't afford to pay you to keep schtum (YET!!!!)

And to my darling Rose, you bring me so much joy I sometimes don't know how to handle it. You are funny (boy are you funny), smart, creative and full of life. The adventures we are going to have my dear, just you watch.

I also have to remind myself that you are also kind and generous, and so forgiving of me not always being with you as much as you would like. You are still my baby right now who needs reassuring, my little girl who looks to me to show you the way...I will never stop striving to be the mum you need me to be.

Know you are loved, and always will be...even when you are 16 and driving me nuts.

These words are never enough. But after 3 months of writing this book they are all I have right now.

If I failed to mention you by name, and you feel excluded I'm sorry...tell me when you see me and I will give you a hug as way of apology. I wrote this bit with hours to spare before the book had to be signed off...what can I say?

To my clients, followers and fans...especially the ladies on my Living a Bigger Life mastermind programme, and my 121 clients who push me to do better.

None of this would have happened without you.

You may be reading this book having been there right from the start, when I was blogging alongside my fulltime job, when I packed and shipped tshirts from my front room...or maybe you came across me more recently...and are completely new to me as an author.

It doesn't matter. You are here and you are part of my world.

We are so much stronger when we are together.

This book is for all of you.

Resources Area

Further Reading

These are a range of books that I have found useful on my own journey, this is of course not an exhaustive list as I read around 100 books a year. Reading has opened my eyes up to so much, but equally I know when to switch off for a bit and just sit with what I already believe to be true.

Health at Every Size: The Surprising Truth About Your Weight, by Linda Bacon
https://amzn.to/2Dvt8vV

Recovery, By Russell Brand **www.amzn.to/2IeU33E**

The Secret by Rhonda Byrne **www.amzn.to/2BWZf6G**

The Big Leap, by Gay Hendricks https://amzn.to/2xS14gr

The universe has your back, by Gabrielle Bernstein **https://amzn.to/2DyRJjx**

Light is the New Black, by Rebecca Campbell https://amzn.to/2xSugE4

Abundance Now, by Lisa Nichols https://amzn.to/2N2DXoX

Get Rich Lucky Bitch by Denise Duffield Thomas **www.amzn.to/2BPrj87**

Rich Dad, Poor Dad by Robert T. Kiyosaki **www.amzn.to/2BQ4vEW**

The Richest Man in Babylon by George S Clason **www.amzn.to/2Ckf1Wm**

The life changing magic of tidy by Marie Kondo **www.amzn.to/2In66LG**

The 5 Love Languages by Gary Chapman **www.amzn.to/2DsAITh**

Will I ever Be Good Enough, by Karyl McBride **www.amzn.to/2BNvbq1**

It Didn't Start with You, by Mark Wolyn **www.amzn.to/2IfgNk3**

Be Happy, by Robert Holden **www.amzn.to/2zJcWA1**

The Power of Now, by Eckhart Tolle **www.amzn.to/2E938Tm**

Web Resources

Many of these web resources are UK based, so please find equivalents in the countries where you are based if not in the UK, although some of the advice may still be relevant

Linda Bacon, the founder of Health at Every Size *https://lindabacon.org/*

Mind, the UKs leading mental health charity **www.mind.org.uk/**

Samaritans, 24 hour counselling and support **www.samaritans.org/**

Heads Together, tackling stigma about mental health **www.headstogether.org.uk**

FREE NHS Health Check **www.nhs.uk/oneyou/hay**

Go Smoke FREE **www.nhs.uk/smokefree**

Club Soda, the mindful drinking movement **www.joinclubsoda.co.uk**

Martin Money Saver, for advice, deals and discounts
www.moneysavingexpert.com

National Debt Advice **www.nationaldebtadvice.org.uk**

Relate, the UKs largest provider of relationship advice **www.relate.org.uk**

The Fat Girls Guide to Running www.toofattorun.co.uk

Ways to Work With Julie Creffield

Coaching

Julie takes on a small number of 121 life coaching clients each year.

She runs an annual Health & Happiness retreat in May in Rhodes, Greece, one day events around the UK and she also runs the following online group programmes.

The Clubhouse – The worlds only plus size online running club
http://www.toofattorun.co.uk/join-the-clubhouse

Stop Dieting, Start Living – An 8-week programme towards self love and acceptance
https://juliecreffield.com/stop-dieting-start-living

Living a Bigger Life – 6 Month Mastermind with Lifetime Access to set and achieve your Big Fat Stupid Goals in life and in business
https://juliecreffield.com/living-a-bigger-life-mastermind/

Book Julie as a Speaker

Julie is an in demand international speaker. As a member of the Professional Speakers Association she speaks on the topics of health, wealth and happiness for women, goal setting and building a global brand, but also on the power of being your true authentic self in life and in business.

She is available for the following kinds of speaking engagements

- Keynotes
- Corporate Events
- After Dinner Speaking
- Conference Activating
- Schools, Colleges and Universities
- Workshops & Training

And has worked with brands such as

- Cancer Research UK
- The National Probation Service
- BritMums Live
- Watertight Marketing
- Stephen Lawrence Trust
- Garmin
- BBC, ITV, Channel 4, Sky News

Please contact **Julie@juliecreffield.com to enquire about availability and rates.**

Printed in Great Britain
by Amazon